Bygone Yetholm

Portrait of a Border Village

A collection of word pictures published by
Yetholm History Society

Printed by Meigle Colour Printers, Tweedbank
2006

ISBN 0-9554149-0-3
ISBN 978-0-9554149-0-9

Bygone Yetholm, the result of more than two years' work, has been compiled and brought to fruition by a study group which consisted of the following members and supporters of Yetholm History Society:

Keith Allbeson
Jenny Angel
Brian Ashby
Janet Campbell
Barbara Goodson
David Hutchinson
Stuart Keddie
Pat Nicolson
Gordon Ogilvie
Jonathan Parsons
Bill Rae
Harry Sangster

• • • • •

Bygone Yetholm
first published in Great Britain in 2006 by Yetholm History Society

ACKNOWLEDGMENTS

Contributions to the book were by no means confined to the members of the study group, listed on a previous page.

Contributors of additional articles include Andy Gray (Yetholm Parish Militia Club), Miss Jean Pinkney (past plant and bird life), Alastair Turnbull (A Childhood in Kirk Yetholm) and Douglas Turnbull (Yetholm Tales). We are particularly grateful to have memoirs by the late Tom Smith, a member of the Society, and the late Isa Nichol.

The original watercolours in the book are by Brian Ashby. The pencil drawings are by Guy Campbell.

The Bygone Yetholm committee also received helpful information from many others, in particular Elma Goodfellow, Ivy Elder, Francis Christie, Tom Tokely, Paul and Sheila Dancey, Jim Dodds, Charles Denoon, and Frank Johnson. Derek Cameron and Kenneth Sibbald both contributed to the story of the Yetholm chicken hatchery. Information about life in the village, and particularly the former YMCA Club, came from Arthur Daw and Webb Daw. Interesting data about the village were found in the 1986 report by the Rev. Joe Brown in the Third Statistical Account of Scotland.

We are grateful to The Southern Reporter, as well as other newspapers and periodicals. The scrapbooks of newspaper cuttings, patiently compiled over many years by the late Mrs Jane Beveridge, is a permanent and convenient source of information,

Others who deserve our thanks include Mrs Jean Robertson, Lottery Officer, Scottish Borders Council, for her advice and encouragement; Awards For All, whose financial support made the book a practical possibility; and Stuart Keddie, for his dedication and patience during the production phase of the book.

Valuable research sources included the Scottish Borders Archive & Local History Centre, Selkirk; the Scottish Department, Edinburgh Central Library; the National Library of Scotland, Edinburgh; the National Archives of Scotland, Edinburgh; and the Royal Commission on the Ancient and Historic Monuments of Scotland, Edinburgh.

For our front cover, a tinted etching that is the oldest known image of Kirk Yetholm, we are indebted to the owner, Mr Alistair Brooks, of the Ednam House Hotel, Kelso. Mr Brooks discovered the etching, which was made about the 1830s, in a shop in Edinburgh. The two-storey buildings in the background were later demolished and replaced by the single-storey houses which remain today. The old Gipsy Palace was rebuilt as Burnsyde House in the late 1880s. That Palace had been the home of Princess Helen, whose older sister, Esther, claimed the throne and moved across the Green to the present Gipsy Palace.

The Queen Inn, also seen in the etching, was owned by King Will Faa II, who was born about 1751 and died in 1847, aged about 95.

The man making the basket is almost certainly John Blithe, the only basket maker in the 1841 Yetholm census. He was an ancestor of Mrs Libby Wichary.

Contents

Introduction

Yetholm occupies an interesting corner of the Scottish collective memory. Ask a group of Scots anywhere what they know about Yetholm, and most of them are likely to mention gipsies. Yet this same group of strangers might struggle to say exactly where this Border village lies, or how they would find their way there.

The fact is that Yetholm's gipsy community, which may have numbered 200 at one time, was assimilated into the local population generations ago. A few of Romany descent still live there, but the gipsy community as such did not survive the nineteenth century.

This gradual dispersal of the gipsies was only one of many social changes to occur. Like every other village in the land, Yetholm's way of life has been transformed in ways that would astonish our grandparents, and perhaps sadden them. Each generation makes its own society.

> "Time, like an ever-rolling stream,
> Bears all her sons away."
> *Isaac Watts (1674-1748)*

And yet photographs that were taken in the main street of Town Yetholm, and of Kirk Yetholm, more than 100 years ago are immediately recognisable. As we examine these faded photographs, there may be a few more thatched roofs, and the trees on the green are much smaller, but the physical shape is much the same today as it was at the birth of photography. Stone is more enduring than social custom.

Old residents brought up in Yetholm recollect that when they were young, there was rather more street activity. This was probably because there were many more village shops then. More people worked locally. The population was younger. There were fewer cars and more pedestrians. The village in 1900 was still close to the self-supporting community it had been for centuries. But that was about to change.

This book does not aspire to be a comprehensive history of Yetholm. Rather it presents a series of pen-pictures, which we hope will convey a flavour of village life as it once was. Wherever possible it tries to tell the story through people rather than institutions, for it is people who make a village.

Chapter 1

In the Long Ago

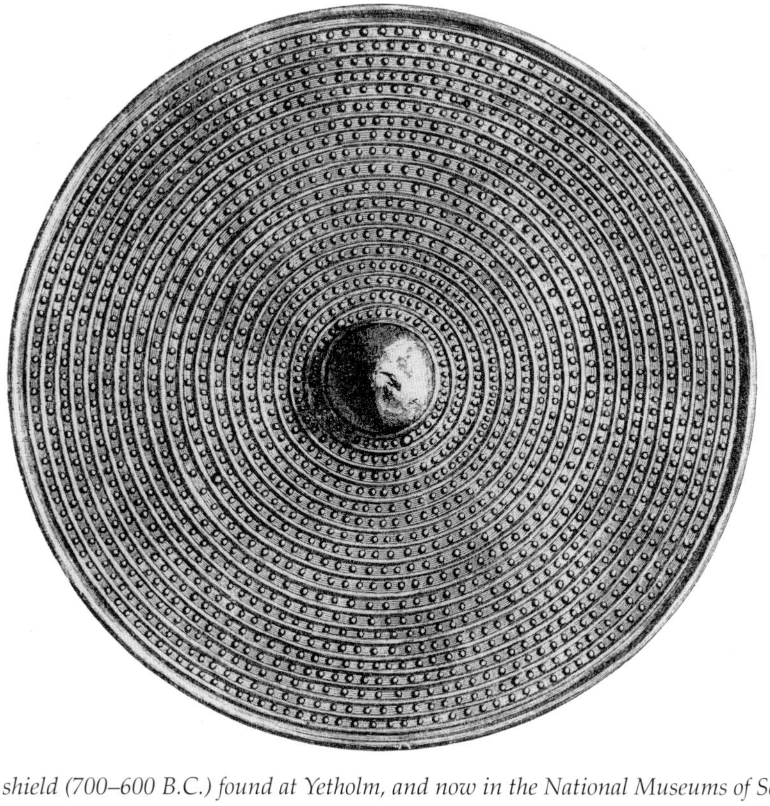

A bronze shield (700–600 B.C.) found at Yetholm, and now in the National Museums of Scotland.

A Rare Encounter

"DURING our morning's tramp [from Kelso to Yetholm] we met a Scotsman, the first we had encountered who would admit there was nothing to interest a stranger in his particular locality, an occurrence so rare that we made a mental note of the fact. Strangely apathetic, indeed, must be the Scotchman whose eyes do not kindle, when speaking about the land of his sires."

Edmund Bogg, in "A Thousand Miles of Wandering in the Border Country", published 1898.

The Very Beginning

As one walks along Yetholm's Main Street on a windswept winter's day, it is hard to appreciate that the land upon which the village is built was formed about 10 degrees south of the Equator.

It is there, about 400 million years ago, that layer upon layer of andesitic lavas – volcanic rock of the type found in the Andes – poured out from a series of volcanoes. It is estimated that these lavas may have attained a height of 5,000 metres.

The present rounded shapes of the low hills we call the Cheviots reflect the weathering and erosion of those 400 million years and the land's tectonic journey from latitude 10 degrees south to 55.5 degrees north.

Looking across at the Cheviots as one descends towards Kelso from Gordon and from Smailholm, the great mass of The Cheviot itself rises lumpily but distinctively almost 300 metres above the surrounding hills.

The reason for its superior height is that it is a vast granite intrusion forced into the older andesitic lava layers. Although it "domed up" the whole area, its rock initially never reached daylight, thereby cooling much more slowly and resulting in much harder rock than the surrounding andesitic lavas.

These andesitic lava layers cooled quickly, becoming much more brittle as a result and, compared to the granite intrusion, they weathered relatively rapidly.

Over millions of years and with four great Ice Ages the softer lava layers wore away, exposing the granite dome we now call The Cheviot.

The last Ice Age, which ground away the evidence of the previous Ice Ages, retreated a mere 10,000 years ago, leaving the Cheviots more or less in their present shape. The most noticeable effect of the melting ice, which can be seen around Yetholm, is the meltwater channel gouged across the north-west side of Yetholm Law. Great underground rivers gouged channels out of the lavas as the main Tweed ice sheet lowered. Other good examples of these meltwater channels can be seen behind the hills from Yeavering Bell, near Kirknewton, down to Humbleton Hill near Wooler, and can be observed from that section of the St Cuthbert's Way walk.

The Return of Vegetation

After the ice melted, leaving bare rock and rubble, vegetation returned. Initially the rock would be colonised by algae and lichens, but eventually the most successful of all plants – the trees – began to cover the area: oak, ash, alder, hazel, etc. These trees probably reached even as high as the summit of The Cheviot.

Two great lakes existed after the retreat of the ice, one covering what is now the Milfield Plain on the Northumbrian side of the Border, and the other stretching from Linton and Morebattle (Mere Bothal, the dwelling by the lake) to Kalemouth. The sand and gravel deposited by the feeder rivers into these post-glacial lakes provide today the Tarmac company at Milfield and Eckford with a thriving extraction business.

From Early Man to the 12th Century

Although Yetholm can boast two of the best Bronze Age finds in Scotland – two magnificent shields found near the Stank below Cherrytrees – the most obvious evidence of early man can be seen in the numerous hill forts. The most readily seen forts are those of the Iron Age (approx. 500 BC until well into the Roman period). Generally speaking, these have two or three ditches and mounds, compared to the more usual single ditch and mound for the Bronze Age forts (approx.1500 BC to 500 BC).

The nearest most obvious Iron Age hill fort is that on Green Humbleton – the hill immediately in front on the road's descent into Halterburn from Yetholm. Walkers on St Cuthbert's Way looking back before reaching the Border line will be able to see the ditches clearly. They will pass a little later the great Votadinian hill fort or town (oppida) of Yeavering Bell, the stone rampart of which can still be seen circling the summit.

Little is known of these people, named by the Romans as the Votadini. Yetholm was then just part of a large area which the Romans controlled, stretching from the Tyne valley to the Firth of Forth. The Votadini appear to have accepted and co-operated with the Romans.

Their neighbouring tribe – the Selgovae – had their territory to the south and west. Seemingly antagonistic to the Romans, they were presumably hostile to the Votadini, and their mutual enmity may well be the cause for the building of so many of the hill forts. The Selgovian capital was on the most northerly of the Eildons above Melrose and their tribal name survives partly in the name, Selkirk.

No evidence of Roman occupation has been discovered in the Yetholm area. However, the great Roman road from Eboracum (York) through Corstopitum (Corbridge on Tyne) over the Cheviots to Trimontium (Newstead, near Melrose) may well have been the boundary between the Votadini and the Selgovae, though this is but surmise. Woden Law above Towford would in that case be a Selgovian fort. It is one of the finest hill forts in the area, complete with practice Roman siege works; it overlooks the Roman infantry temporary camps at Pennymuir, which are the best preserved group of marching camps in Scotland.

The Roman legions were withdrawn from Britain in 410 AD and thereafter legend (and an ever increasing body of archaeological evidence) takes over until the monks of Lindisfarne, Jarrow and Durham make written records during the Anglo Saxon period.

From Northumbrian Settlement to Scottish Border Village

DURING the 7th century the Yetholm area (previously settled by the 'Votadinian' Britons) became part of the Kingdom of Northumbria, which at this time began to emerge as the most powerful military and civilising unit in Britain. The Kingdom reached from the Humber to the Firth of Forth and beyond in the east, and to the Solway in the west.

One detailed account of the Yetholm area at this time comes much later from a monk, Symeon of Durham (1060-1130) who records that before the year 670 King Oswy of Northumbria granted to the monks of Lindisfarne (Holy Island) all the lands of the Bowmont Water together with the hamlets of Sourhope, Staerough, Morebattle, Clifton, Halterburn, Thornington, Shotton, Yetholm and Mindrum.

By the early 10th century Northumbrian power had begun to wither and wane. Battered by Viking raids since their attack on Lindisfarne in 793, pressed from the north and west by the growing power of the Gaelic-speaking Kings of Alba, the Northumbrians lost control of the Lothians.

In 1018 Malcolm II, King of the Picts and Scots, defeated the Anglian forces at Carham and thereafter, save for the final loss of Berwick to the English in 1482, the far eastern Border line became established from the Redden Burn's junction with the Tweed just beyond Sprouston to the mouth of the Tweed.

In its introduction the Royal Commission on Ancient and Historic Monuments, Roxburghshire volume, states: "In the 7th century, however, the human stock was unquestionably profoundly modified by the Anglian settlement, the results of which modification have persisted throughout the succeeding centuries. English for example has remained the predominating language… and it is consequently natural, as it is no doubt also correct in a general way, to regard the medieval and later inhabitants as essentially English."

Whereas the Border line between Malcolm II's Scots and the Northumbrians remained fixed at the Tweed north-east of Redden, the Border to the south-west and over the Cheviots was to remain in dispute for centuries.

It is difficult to assess when Yetholm changed from being a part of Anglian Northumbria to a Scottish possession. In reality, Scotland as a unified nation in itself did not come into being until the Pictish people had been absorbed by the Scots; the Vikings (Norwegians) were ousted after the Battle of Largs in 1263; and the Norman-style barons like King David I and the Bruces were threatened by Edward I of England.

Alexander III (1249-1286), who brought about a 'Golden Age' in Scotland, was Edward I's brother-in-law. Trade flourished, Berwick grew into the commercial capital of Scotland, and a centralised and effective form of government was established; relations with England were wary but friendly. Two sons and a daughter secured the succession.

In 1275, however, an inexorable tragedy began to unfold. In that year Alexander's wife (Edward I's sister) died. In 1281 his youngest son died, followed by his daughter, the Queen of Norway. Then his eldest son died. The succession gone, Alexander married again, but in 1286, travelling one stormy night from south of the Forth to see his young wife at Kinghorn, his horse slipped in the darkness. He was thrown over the cliffs and killed. A further twist to the tragedy was yet to come. His grand-daughter in Norway was the sole survivor of his family, but in 1290 at the age of seven on her way over to Scotland, she too died.

After Alexander's death Edward I, having secured Wales by force, had been negotiating the annexation of Scotland by more peaceful means: the marriage of his son to Alexander's Norwegian grand-daughter. With her death, however, Edward moved rapidly by infiltration and manoeuvre to fill the power vacuum that had occurred. In doing so he ignited a latent but incipient Scottish national identity. The ensuing conflagration was to have catastrophic results for both nations. Yetholm was to find itself on the front line of that conflict for the next 300 years. By the Union of the Crowns in 1603, however, Yetholm was firmly one and a half miles north of the Border.

Turbulent Times

Every village has a story to tell. Few places are too small or remote not to have been influenced by the politics, fashions or disadvantages of the world about it, and Yetholm got off to a cracking start, hardly born before achieving the rare distinction of having its name appear in manuscript as early as 655, when King Oswy gave it away to the Church.

In that year, there would still have been some alive to remember and speak of the great ingathering of people from the surrounding countryside for the mass baptisms by the priest Paulinus, brought to them 28 years earlier by another King. Total immersion in the chill water of the River Glen, a thoroughly uncomfortable business, was not likely to be forgotten, even if the new fashion for one God may have slipped a bit; though no doubt once the monks were running things the idea would have taken a stronger grip.

Quite when there came to be a church building in Yetholm is unknown, but the first mention of one is in 1233, together with its Rector, Nicholas de Glenwyn. There is little on record between Oswy's gift and Nicholas' first sermon, other than a few land transfers, but other significant events must have taken place. It is quite possible that Yetholm was affected by one, or both of the two great 9th century invasions into the Lothians by those feared and heathen people, the Vikings of York, and maybe the villages integrated with later Norse settlers. Evidence for these events, albeit scanty, exists in the form of Norse burial stones close to Lempitlaw and Ancrum, and two hoards of Viking hack silver found in the Tweed Basin.

In 1295 the then Rector of Yetholm, seen as a reliable man, was asked to act on behalf of the Abbot of Dunfermline in a dispute with the monks of Kelso Abbey. In 1296, when "Mestre Walran", rector, swore fealty to King Edward I he had his lands restored to him, the rectory then being valued at 53s 4d per annum.

In 1304, Edward I camped at Yetholm for three days where, having "made peace" with certain Scottish "rebels", he formally restored their land to them in a charter dated from "Yetham" on 24th August.

In 1368 King Edward III charged the Sheriff of Roxburgh (then occupied by the English) to take care that no clergyman other than the one he had appointed, John of "Alnewyk" be admitted, though the Bishop of Glasgow had refused to induct him: six years later the King gave it to somebody else anyway, John Walweyes, who apparently (one wonders why) didn't like it, since he very shortly exchanged to Minto.

In the 1350s, unrecorded so far as Yetholm is concerned, but very much present, there was something else of significance. *"God and Sen Mungo, Sen Ninian and Seynt Andrew scheld us this day and ilka day fro Goddis grace and the foule deth that Ynglessh men dyene upon"* may well have been the prayer in Yetholm church. It certainly was for the Scots army who, it is recorded, were at first delighted by the fate overtaking their enemies. But *"it was sayd, of lyvand men the thyrd part it dystroyid, then efftyr that [it was] in till Scotland a yhere or more"*. Which must have wiped the smile from their faces and makes it unlikely that Yetholm was unaffected.

In 1388 the Earl of Douglas mustered his army in Yetholm before marching down to defeat the English under Henry Percy of Northumberland. Percy was taken prisoner, but Douglas was killed.

In 1401, a meeting was held within Yetholm church to negotiate a truce between the two countries. The words used by the English to describe the Scottish attitude in their report were "aggressive" and "antagonistic" for it seems a tulzie broke out, actual bloodshed being averted only by the courteous intervention of a cleric (our Rector?). One can imagine the gossip that night, and for many more, in the medieval equivalents of the Border Inn and the Plough.

In 1513 Yetholm must have felt the effects of Flodden, though it is highly unlikely that bodies were brought to the village in any quantity for burial. Most corpses in such events went into mass graves on site, while those considered to be of more importance were taken home.

In 1523 the Earl of Surrey lodged his men *"near unto a fortress called Lough Towre, whiche, in the morning before sonne rising was clerely throwen down and rased, with the devises accustomed"* before going on to burn Linton and Cessford.

A century later "Kirkyethame" was a frequent meeting place for the negotiations between the Wardens of the respective Marches, though towards the end of the 16th century the Scottish Warden of the Middle Marches, Kerr of Cessford, seemed to have had a very laid-back attitude to his duties, because in 1586 he put the meeting off three times, twice claiming engagements elsewhere, and the third time apparently because he didn't want to get wet, misliking "of the vehemencie of the wether" (it was March), he suggested that "the dayis may be keipit by our deputies."

In 1596, however, there was some business dealt with. In Cessford's "Roll of Wrongs" a note of the *"slauchters, stowthis and reiffis as has bene committet be the inhabitants of the Eist Wardarnye of England"* there was, among others, one from the tenants of "Yettem", complaining of a raid "in daylight" by Roger Gray, bailiff of Berwick and the rest of Mr Raulf Grayes household men, 20 persons, who were said to have driven away 24 horses and mares. To which complaint came smartly a reply from the English Warden that it was an" untroth" and that the horses of the "Yettam" tenants were lawfully taken, in English ground, whilst carrying away wood. So there!

Neither was restitution ever made for the alleged lifting of 3,500 sheep and 500 nolt (cattle) from Yetholm and Kirk Yetholm by Musgrave of Harbottle Castle one summer's day, on the ground that it was done by order of the English Warden. Who knows? Perhaps it was really only 35 sheep and 5 cows; in such matters neither side ever resisted gross exaggeration – not if there was money in it.

The two villages may have also experienced the legitimate passage of other cattle. The Union saw an increase in the droving trade and, as the Napoleonic Wars sent the price of beef up to nearly double that of 50 years before, the herds coming from all the airts grew more frequent and took a greater variety of routes, so that Yetholm may well have seen some of them. Noisy, smelly herds filling up the spaces between the houses, and grief for those women who didn't get their front doors firmly snecked as the beasts went jostling and lowing down the street: few things are so awkward as a frightened cow in the kitchen.

Ancient Shields Unearthed

A MAN digging to improve the drainage of the marshy field then called Yetholm Bog, beyond where the playing field now stands, suddenly struck two objects which must be the most interesting ever unearthed in the village.

It was in the spring of 1837, and the objects were bronze shields. Each was approximately 24 inches in diameter, and ornamented with concentric rows of small convex studs or knobs, alternating with projecting circles or ribs. In the centre of each shield was a projecting circular boss, 4 inches across. On the inner side, across the hollow boss, was a bronze handle, fastened by rivets. Experts dated the shields to 700-600 B.C.

Shortly after their discovery they were exhibited by Mr George Wauchope of Niddry, at a meeting of the Society of Antiquaries of Scotland on 10 April 1837.

Bronze shields of the same type had been found elsewhere in Britain, but the Yetholm discovery was only the second recorded in Scotland.

There was a sequel to the story. Thirty three years later, on 19 March 1870, a third bronze shield was found by a man ploughing in the same field, not far from the Stank.

The historian Alexander Jeffrey, who was a Jedburgh solicitor, reported to the Society of Antiquaries of Scotland that the third shield was found about ten inches from the surface, standing on edge, in the direction of east and west. It was very similar in size and design to the two found earlier. All three also had tongues of bronze, probably for the attachment of a leather strap by which to sling the shield around the body.

Bronze suggests such shields may have belonged to chiefs and for that reason were buried with them. The shields are now in the Museum of Scotland, in Edinburgh.

We are fortunate to have the shields: Sir Samuel Meyrick reported to the Society of Antiquaries of London that one such shield was found near Newcastle-on-Tyne, but the owner, wishing to oblige his friends, had it cut up like a cake, so that each might have a slice.

Our Oldest Tree

THE oldest living thing in Yetholm is the yew tree which stands off Yewtree Lane, on the edge of the allotments.

This majestic tree is thought to be anywhere between 300 and 500 years old, and may have been planted to mark where victims of a plague were buried in the 1660s. It has attracted the attention of the Borders Forest Trust, which implemented in 1997 a regional veteran tree project, which aims to locate old and ancient trees. The Trust promotes their conservation. Yew trees, which are often planted in churchyards, can live 1,000 years.

Their leaves are poisonous. Some years ago, the lower branches of the Yetholm Tree had to be cut back after a Clydesdale horse chewed one or two branches and died. There was another recorded incident in the distant past when some pigs died after eating a mash that had been merely stirred with a branch from the tree.

It is the subject of a Tree Preservation Order, and permission would have to be obtained from Scottish Borders Council to have it felled.

Chapter 2

Some Historic Landowners

The Wauchopes of Niddrie

The Wauchope family, whose descendants were to become the principal landowners in Yetholm, first appear in the history books about 600 years ago. Their earliest estate was at Niddrie, a district that is now within Edinburgh, but which at that period was in the depths of rural Midlothian. In the following centuries, Wauchopes played prominent roles in many of the turbulent events of Scottish and British history, the family producing a succession of churchmen, soldiers, political conspirators, desperadoes and religious scholars[1].

The Edinburgh chapter of the Wauchope story came to an end not long after the Second World War, when the Niddrie estate was absorbed by the expanding City of Edinburgh.

The family has had a connection with Yetholm since 1661. How did this come about? In the 16th century the barony of Lochtour had belonged to the Earl of Bothwell, husband of Mary, Queen of Scots, but in 1563, before his forfeiture, he disposed of Lochtour to the Ker family.

In 1661 the head of the Wauchope family was Sir John Wauchope, who seems to have been a shrewd individual where money was concerned A history of the family states that Sir John exercised great judgment in the management

[1] Probably the most famous of the scholars was Robert Wauchope (died 1551). Virtually blind from birth, he possessed extraordinary talents. He was sent to Paris University, where he was Doctor of Divinity and was elected Procurator eight times. The Pope appointed him legate to Germany and France, and Wauchope attended the entire Council of Trent, dying shortly thereafter in Paris.

of his estate and, in course of time, more than rectified damage that had been sustained by his father, Sir Francis Wauchope.

The ancient barony of Lochtour was owned at this time by Sir Gilbert Ker. However, Sir John was owed considerable money by Sir Gilbert, this money having been advanced by Wauchope at least 17 years earlier. In the legal jargon of the period, Wauchope had a wadset of 25,000 merks over the lands of Lochtour.

Sir Gilbert was in debt not only to Sir John but all over the place. He was, in fact, overwhelmed with debt and law expenses, and it became impossible for him to retain his property. The Wauchope family history puts it thus: "Overdue bonds, in numerous quarters, kept pouring their legal streams incessantly against him."

A number of these debts had been paid by Sir John, or had been purchased by him. The take-over came in 1661. Sir John and his wife had been guests at the coronation of Charles II; and on their way home, no doubt in a state of pleasant euphoria, they dropped in at Lochtour and talked over the situation with the financially embarrassed Sir Gilbert Ker. As we might say today, Sir John must have made him an offer he could not refuse, and a price for Lochtour was agreed.

A decade later, in 1672, the property is described as consisting of "the lands and barony of Niddrie-Merschell and all the lands, toune and maynes of the baronie of Tounyettoum, with the milne, milne lands, multures and sequills[2] thereof..." The property also included the right of patronage of the kirk of Yetholm.

The agreement did not end the legal arguments. Years later Sir John's son, Andrew Wauchope, found himself the defender in protracted lawsuits, brought against him first by his half-brother and then by members of the Ker family. It was a wrangle about inheritance and control of the barony, and the court eventually found in favour of the Wauchopes.

The evidence given during the legal action provides a striking illustration of how business three centuries ago was conducted. By now, Sir John Wauchope and Sir Gilbert Ker were both dead, and so the court took the testimony of a servant who had been in the employ of Sir John 30 years earlier.

[2] Multures and sequels were the fees and allowances payable between a mill owner and grain farmers who were thirled (i.e. legally bound) to use a certain mill.

This servant described a meeting held by the Wauchopes and the Kers in the Black Bull in Edinburgh: this was a famous tavern which stood in the Royal Mile of the Old Town. The servant related how he and others had carried "many baggs of money" into the meeting, to be handed over to Lady Ker in settlement of the business transaction.

That was how deals had to be settled in those days, because in Scotland there were as yet no banks. (Incidentally, a young Scotsman named William Paterson did start a bank – but to do so he had to go to London, where the big money was: Paterson called his venture the Bank of England).

Tragic End of A General

"When the General was killed at Magersfontein in the South African War, the village mourned him deeply... I can remember the time when nearly every house had a picture or photo of 'the General', as he was affectionately called. It was always given a place of honour in the home."

Major-General Andrew Wauchope.

So wrote the late Isa Nichol of Major-General Andrew Gilbert Wauchope, the laird of Yetholm and the most famous member of the landowning family, the Wauchopes of Niddrie. He was also one of the richest men in Scotland.

The General's name keeps cropping up regularly as one researches Yetholm in the 19th century. As the local laird, he seems to have been a man with the interests of the community at heart. He provided the first piped supply of water to the village, where several now redundant street wells still stand.

Andrew Gilbert Wauchope was born in 1846, the third child of Andrew Wauchope, landowner, and his wife Frances Mary. She was an Irish lady from Tippereray. Evidently known to his friends as "Andy", Wauchope was a brave and dedicated soldier, and saw much active service.

An unusual feature of his career was that he was at first in the Royal Navy: he was a midshipman at the age of 14, but obtained his discharge two years later. He joined the Army and was commissioned into the Black Watch at the age of 19. Wauchope saw service in Cyprus in 1878, and in 1882, when the Royal Navy bombarded Alexandria and landed an expeditionary force, Wauchope took part in the decisive Battle of Tel el-Kebir. There are many anecdotes in a biography[1] to show that he was a caring and popular officer.

In Sudan, as commander of the Highland Brigade at the Battle of Omdurman in September 1898, he played an important part in that victory, and in gratitude Sir Hector Macdonald presented Wauchope with the Khalifa's captured flag. Sir Herbert Kitchener rewarded Wauchope with an elephant's tusk. Both of these trophies were displayed for many years inthe lofty entrance hall of the family mansion at Niddrie Marischal, on the outskirts of Edinburgh. It was in 1898 that Wauchope was promoted to Major-General.

Omdurman, however, lay several months in the future when the Colonel attended in Yetholm the induction ceremonies of the Rev. William Carrick Miller. Wauchope's regiment at the time was stationed in Yorkshire, and he cleared his desk there at midnight and dashed north immediately, in time to attend the induction service in the parish church at noon. He then took the chair at the traditional lunch, held in the Border Hotel immediately afterwards. No doubt the Colonel felt it his duty to attend these ceremonies: he was an elder of the Church of Scotland as well as principal heritor of Yetholm (as such he had a say in the choice of parish minister). Incidentally, the lunch in the Border Hotel was followed by no fewer than 18 toasts, replies or other speeches before the company dispersed. That evening there was a soiree at the church, attended by about 600, and the Colonel was again among the speakers.

At the Border Hotel lunch, after the guests had stood up and sung "For he's a jolly good fellow", Colonel Wauchope made a patriotic speech. These years were, of course, the zenith of the British Empire. During his remarks Colonel Wauchope referred to a recent campaign on the north-west frontier of India, and the courageous part played in it by Scottish regiments. He suggested that, in order to ensure the supremacy of the Empire, the time had come when the nation would have to make up its mind for a large increase in the strength of our army, and the pay of the men serving in the ranks would also have to be increased (Hear, hear, and applause).[2]

---

1 William Baird. *General Wauchope* Edinburgh 1902

2 Kelso Mail, 23 February 1898

The Wauchope Memorial is unveiled.

A year after the celebration of Mr Miller's induction came the South African War. The Battle of Magersfontein, in which Wauchope was killed while leading the Highland Brigade against the Boer lines, was one of the early defeats sustained by the British during the three-year conflict. It was devastating news, and was felt far beyond Yetholm, for the Highland Brigade as a whole suffered grievously at the hands of the expert Boer sharpshooters.

There is evidence of Wauchope's personal popularity in a letter to the Editor of "The Scotsman", written in 1937: this was, remember, many years after Wauchope's death. In his letter, a Mr Thomas Thomson recalled:

"It must be over 40 years since the citizens of Edinburgh used to watch, with a thrill of pride in their hearts, the regiment of the Black Watch, swinging along Princes Street on a fine sunny morning, with Colonel Wauchope lean and bronzed, with a serious, shrewd and kindly face, his blue eyes seeing everything, mounted at their head. How Wauchope was loved by everybody! His men adored him, and he was proud of his men."[3]

Is Mr Thomas Thomson, in expressing this admiring personal view, carried away? Was Wauchope shrewd? Did he enjoy the adoration of his men?

---

[3] The Scotsman, 1937

Perhaps he did. But there is a dissenting view. A poem, written by a survivor of Magersfontein, expresses criticism of the British leadership. Can Wauchope be held primarily responsible for this costly and painful defeat? Wauchope was under the orders of the British commander, Lord Methuen. It was Methuen who, having been given instructions to raise the siege of the "diamond town", Kimberley, resolved to make a frontal attack upon the Boer stronghold on the Magersfontein ridge. One account[4] states that Wauchope had asked that the Highland Brigade of four battalions be allowed to outflank the ridge, but this was refused by Methuen. Before making the attack, Methuen shelled the Boer position with all his artillery, including a great naval gun. One view is that the artillery bombardment was too brief, and was directed upon the summit of the ridge when in fact the Boer trenches had been dug below the ridge.[5]

It was a night attack. Wauchope's advance began shortly after midnight on 11th December 1899, and took place during cold and heavy rain, and a dark so intense that the men had to move on compass bearing and guided by ropes. Wauchope was in the leading file. In atrocious conditions of driving rain, thorns, uneven muddy ground, and obliged to hold on to each other for direction, they succeeded in covering less than five miles before the sky began to lighten, at which time one of Wauchope's officers stated that in his opinion it was no longer safe to advance or to deploy and advised withdrawal. However, the advance continued.

They were pushing through a dense belt of thorns when, in the words of a survivor, the ground "seemed to explode... it was lit up, as if someone had turned on a million electric lights..." At a range of no more than 400 yards, the Boers opened fire from a long line of trenches that lay, not on the bombarded ridge, but on the front below the summit.

A verse written by a survivor, a private of the Black Watch, asks poignantly:

"Why weren't we told of the trenches?
Why weren't we told of the wire?
Why were we marched up in column?
May Tommy Atkins enquire....

"Dearly we paid for the blunder
A drawingroom General's mistake."[6]

---

[4] The Scotsman, 11 December 1999

[5] William Baird. op. cit.

[6] Thomas Pakenham. *The Boer War* (London 1979)

Wauchope, 18 of his officers, and about 750 men were killed in the hesitation and shock of that fire. A further 200 survivors and wounded were picked off by snipers as they lay in the heat of a long day before they were able to withdraw.

The memorial to Wauchope on Town Yetholm green was raised by public subscription and unveiled about three years after his death.

Marquesses of Tweeddale

For approximately 200 years, from the 18th century until the first half of the 20th, the major landed proprietors in Kirk Yetholm were the Marquesses of Tweeddale.

Rather more than fifty years ago, however, the Tweeddale family sold the lands of Yetholm Mains and Halterburn, and the smaller farm of Yetholm Mill. By 1952 the author of the Third Statistical Account, the Rev. Kenneth MacFadden, could report that Lord Tweeddale now owned no land in Yetholm parish.

The family name is Hay. The Hays are originally from East Lothian, the family seat being at Yester, near Haddington. They were not resident proprietors in Yetholm, a fact that was remarked upon on more than one occasion by the parish ministers when they wrote up the Statistical Accounts.

The Hays are a very old Scottish family, for they can trace their lineage back to a Sir John de Haya, in the 13th century. Their earliest recorded connection with the Borders occurs in the 14th century, when a Sir William de Haya was Sheriff of Peebles.

There is an interesting event in the early 1500s, when a member of the family, Beatrice Hay, married a William Wauchope, younger, of Niddrie Marischal: this is the earliest record of a marriage union between the two families who were to become influential proprietors in this part of Roxburghshire.

From at least the Battle of Flodden, in September 1513 (where the head of the Hay family was killed), the Hays played an active and prominent part in the political, religious and military history of Scotland and Britain. Their name crops up regularly in the affairs of state, during the time of Mary, Queen of Scots; Charles I; Oliver Cromwell; Charles II; and the Covenanting period.

Beyond these shores, it was a similar story. A succession of Hays saw active service in China, India, Spain, Canada and America: in every military campaign, it seems, there was a Hay – either in the Army or in the Royal Navy.

At home in Scotland, in the 18th and 19th centuries, the Hays were also noted agricultural improvers. Of John Hay, the 4th Marquess of Tweeddale, one authority[1] states: "By him the estate of Yester was greatly improved, particularly in the way of enclosing fields and planting trees, and towards the close of the 18th century the estate contained some of the finest timber in Scotland."

How did the Tweeddale connection with Kirk Yetholm come about? The definitive history of Roxburghshire[1] suggests that, on the death of Captain David Bennet, the proprietor of the barony of Yetholm (and the Yetholm gipsies' famous champion) he was succeeded by Nisbet of Dirleton. Following Nisbet of Dirleton's death, the estate at Kirk Yetholm was purchased by the trustees of the Marquess of Tweeddale.

The 8th Marquess, George Hay, was in the Army and attained the rank of Field-Marshal. When he retired in 1848 he returned to Yester. "He led the way in tile-draining, in deep ploughing, and in many bold experiments… He also showed an intelligent interest… in mechanics, where his knowledge enabled him to invent machinery which has been found useful by farmers."[1] He was elected president of the Agricultural and Highland Society (as it was then called). It is not clear whether his experiments and innovations were confined to the main estate in East Lothian, or whether these benefits were extended to his lands at Kirk Yetholm.

The 8th Marquess must have been an impressive character. "He was a man of conspicuous physique, and celebrated in the army as a horseman and sabreur. He was also an accomplished coachman, and is said to have once driven the mail from London to Haddington without a halt or relief." The Marquess died from an accident in 1876, at the age of 89. [2]

---

[1] Alexander Jeffrey. *History and Antiquities of Roxburghshire* Edinburgh 1859.

[2] Dictionary of National Biography

Chapter 3

The Gipsies from 1505 to 1898

The Gipsies Arrive in Scotland

No one knows for certain when gipsies first entered Scotland. The earliest written record appears to be an entry in the books of the Lord High Treasurer for 22 April 1505, at the court of King James IV. This was a small payment to gipsies, probably for providing entertainment.

Where are the gipsies from? It is now thought that this mysterious people came originally from India, and that in the 1400s they began a slow migration overland westwards.

Many people have found similarities between Romany words and their equivalent in Hindustani, and evidence of this is presented elsewhere in this book. The gipsies passed through eastern Europe, Germany and France and eventually landed in England. They then gradually moved north into Scotland.

As an ethnic minority, with distinctly separate customs and following a nomadic way of life, perhaps it was inevitable that in every country in which the gipsies settled, they gradually attracted suspicion, which sometimes developed into outright hostility. In England, for example, Henry VIII went so far as to try to banish all gipses back to the Continent.

In Scotland, the relationship was uneasy at the best of times; and in bad times, the gipsies were actively persecuted. In the early 1600s, the Scottish Privy Council issued a number of decrees which banished the whole race from Scotland, under pain of death. It was lawful for anyone to apprehend and execute any gipsies who might be found within the country.

Fortunately for the gipsies, law enforcement was patchy, communications being poor, and large tracts of country were almost inaccessible. That was one reason why gipsies settled in Kirk Yetholm. Another reason was the proximity of the Border between Scotland and England; if things became too hot, they could move over into a different jurisdiction.

Smuggling (which, of course, was not confined to the gipsies) was a flourishing industry in Yetholm; it has been claimed that at one time, one in five of the entire local population was making a living from this form of illegal trading.

The Gipsies' Champion

While no one can say when the first gipsy entered Yetholm, the year 1695 is generally accepted as the beginning of the modern chapter of this long association. In that year at the siege of Namur, in what is now Belgium, the life of a British officer, Captain David Bennet, was saved by a gipsy comrade-in-arms named Young.

Bennet owned land in Yetholm, being proprietor of the barony, and in gratitude he made cottages freely available to his saviour, other gipsies and their descendants.

Some fifty years later, probably the best known gipsy in Scotland was Jean Gordon, who evidently was born in Yetholm about 1670 and whose strong personality inspired Sir Walter Scott to create the character of Meg Merrilees in his novel, "Guy Mannering". Jean, an ardent Jacobite, met a violent death in Carlisle in 1746 when she was ducked in the river by an anti-Jacobite mob.

Bennet's successor was a relation, Nisbet of Dirleton, and later the land was purchased by the Marquesses of Tweeddale.

Kirk Yetholm, 1817

A visitor about 1817 found distinct differences between Town Yetholm and Kirk Yetholm. In the former, he noticed the little cultivated enclosures we now know as the Loanings.

"Town-Yetholm lies rather low, and exhibits nothing remarkable either in the character of its inhabitants or its internal appearance; but a small conical hill, whose rocky summit retains the vestiges of some ancient entrenchments, rises between it and Loch-Tower, and presents a very pleasing view on approaching from the north. It is cultivated on all sides quite to the top – and the small village-tenants, by whom it is chiefly occupied, have parcelled out its sloping declivities into parks, or little enclosures, of almost Chinese variety – each of which exhibits, on a small scale, the diversified operations and variegated vegetation of Scottish husbandry.

"The aspect of the opposite village, to which the gipsy population is entirely confined, is of a different character: a mill and a churchyard rising from the brink of the water – the church itself low and covered with thatch – beyond which appear the straggled houses of the village, built in the old Scottish style, many of them with their gable-ends, backs, or corners, turned to the street or toun-gate – and still farther up, the Tinkler-Row, with its low, unequal, straw-covered roofs, and chimneys bound with rushes and hay-ropes – men and women loitering at their doors – and ragged children scrambling on the midden-steads (which rise before every cottage) in intimate and equal fellowship with pigs, poultry, dogs and cuddies."[1]

---

[1] Blackwood's Edinburgh Monthly Magazine, vol I, issue II: May 1817 pp43–58.

Minister with a Mission

More than any other individual, the Rev. John Baird was to play a decisive role in the destiny of the Yetholm gipsies. Baird, who had been appointed Church of Scotland parish minister at Yetholm in 1829, became aware about ten years later of missionary work being done to support gipsies in southern England. He decided it was his duty to publish a local scheme to carry out similar work in Kirk Yetholm.

Baird's scheme was designed to promote better relations between employers and the gipsy community; to provide tools, furniture and books; and, most significant of all, to persude the nomadic gipsies to allow their children to remain in Yetholm and go to school. The acceptance by gipsy parents of the notion that their children would benefit from a classroom education was to prove a watershed in the history of the Yetholm gipsies.

Baird was born in 17 February 1799 at the manse of Eccles, Berwickshire, where his father was parish minister. As a young man he made a 12-month sea voyage for his health, and as a result became well known as a botanist and geologist. His work on behalf of the gipsies was done with the help of a society that had been formed in Edinburgh for the "Reformation of the Gypsies in Scotland". He did not find it an easy task, particularly in the early years. The key was his continuing efforts to educate and promote the care of the gipsy children; the school which he established for them in Yetholm was the first "Ragged School" in Scotland.

John Baird died at the manse in Kirk Yetholm on 29 November 1861, aged 62, and is buried in the churchyard.

The Redoubtable Queen Esther

The lady known to history as "the last Queen of the Gipsies", Esther Faa Blythe, succeeded to the title after her father, Charles Blythe, died in 1861 at the age of about 83.

We have a pen-portrait of Queen Esther by an anonymous writer[1] in an issue of Chambers' Journal, who visited her in Kirk Yetholm some four years before her death in 1883. Esther, who by then was more than 80, was wearing a scrupulously neat dress, with silvery hair beneath an antique linen cap. The writer describes Esther as a remarkable woman in many respects, with a deep knowledge of human character. The conversation was of the crops, poaching, the St. James's fairs in former times, and reminiscences of travel on the old Roman roads.

Queen Esther could suit her conversation to her visitors and, if it were called for, could employ a keen sarcasm. She did not claim to have the gift of fortune-telling. Queen Esther was a welcome guest in the houses of the nobility and gentry; she had a fund of gipsy stories.

In early life Esther had married John Rutherford, of Jedburgh ("Jethart Jock"), but was a widow for many years. There were 12 children of the marriage, of whom five sons and three daughters survived her. Esther became Queen only by contesting the matter. When her father died in 1861 he should have been succeeded by his son, David, but David did not want the throne and waived his right in favour of his youngest sister, Princess Helen.

---

[1] Chambers' Journal, 18 August 1883 pp 518-520

Queen Esther, who reigned from 1861 until her death in 1883, was a formidable character, quite capable of holding her own in any conversation with distinguished visitors.

However, Esther, who was the eldest sister, now asserted a claim. She had never admitted her father's right to the crown, on the ground that he was not a Faa.

Did the dispute come to blows? Legend says that the issue of succession was settled by a fight between the two rival claimants on the green. This is possible, given that the gipsy community had a tradition of settling internal disputes in such a way. We know more about Queen Esther, an acknowledged formidable personality, than we do about her sister Princess Helen, a more shadowy figure. So a physical clash is a possibility, perhaps even likely. But on the other hand it may have been no more than a noisy verbal exchange in public, which became exaggerated in the re-telling.

Esther issued a proclamation dated 1 November 1861, which summoned all the members of the various tribes to witness her coronation at Kirk Yetholm on Tuesday, 12 November 1861. There was no further dispute.

The coronation took place on Kirk Yetholm green at the cross (the base of which can just be traced in the grass to this day). A large number of the various gipsy tribes were present, and the Queen was attended by Princes and Princesses. The crowning ceremony was performed by the village blacksmith, George Gladstone, acting in his honorary capacity as "Archbishop" to the royal house. The Queen thanked her subjects for placing her upon the throne of her ancestors, and hoped that they would live at peace with all men. Her Majesty later held a levee.

Queen Esther died at Kelso in July 1883. She was buried at Yetholm, in the presence of a large multitude, beside her husband. Their graves are no longer marked, but are believed to lie a few yards to the right as one enters the churchyard gate.

A period of 15 years was to elapse before the celebrated coronation of her son, Charles Faa Blythe, at Kirk Yetholm on 30 May 1898. This was to prove a spectacular affair, attended by an estimated 10,000 people.

The Gipsy Palace

For at least 200 years, and probably much longer, Kirk Yetholm was regarded by gipsies as their headquarters for the whole of Scotland and North of England. They were congregated in a mixter-maxter collection of thatched cottages which stood at the top of the village, on each side of the street known as Tinklers' Row. The winter population may have been in the region of 200.

The reigning King (or Queen) had their official abode in a cottage which came to be called, with some irony, the royal palace.

The present Gipsy Palace is not the original: there was an earlier palace, a thatched cottage no longer in existence, which occupied a site nearby but on the other side of the road.

This earlier palace survived until the late nineteenth century, and is described by a writer in Blackwood's Magazine in 1898 as a one-roomed cottage with a primitive floor of clay and an old-fashioned open fireplace from which the smoke ascended through a hole in the roof. One of the last occupants of this earlier cottage was Princess Helen, the youngest sister of the celebrated Queen Esther Faa Blythe.

The present palace was occupied by, among others, Queen Esther (died Kelso, 1883) and the last monarch, Esther's son, Charles Faa Blythe (died 1902). Esther was a formidable personality who was visited by a number of well-known figures, with whom she more than held her own in conversation.

Departed Chiefs

"We looked into the kirkyard to see the tombstones and graves of the departed chiefs and their consorts, almost hidden in the long grass, descendants of a long line of Romanies who, in the flight of centuries, in their migration westward, reached this spot from the Far East.

"There are several theories, but there seems little doubt as to their origin, as a great many words in their vocabulary, their nomadic habits, their love of horse-dealing, fortune-telling, and palmistry, are all indicative of their descent from the caste of Central India, known as Doms."

Edmund Bogg: *"A Thousand Miles of Wandering in the Border Country" (1898), pp 211-215*

Chapter 4

Yetholm's Farming Economy

The Agriculture Revolution

Before the Treaty of Union of 1707, the condition of agriculture in Scotland would have presented to moden eyes a bleak picture indeed. Farming was based upon the ancient run-rig system, which involved community cultivation of strips of land of varying quality. Farms were small, pasture land was not artificially enhanced, stock rearing methods were primitive, there was a lack of tree shelter, and drainage of the land was little more than that wrought by Nature.

Prior to the enclosure movement, farming was a matter of subsistence for the individual farmer and his family; after enclosure, farming became a matter of selling, of trade, of profit and loss, of prosperity and recession. Yetholm could not be insulated from such national trends.

This agrarian revolution, which progressed over a considerable period, took two forms: a series of technical improvements – rotation of crops, new crops, new implements – and the gradual replacement of the immemorial system of run-rig and open fields. With the benefit of hindsight, the revolution in the countryside can be seen as having been inevitable, owing to its link with the industrial revolution and the growth of British cities, where an increasing population was creating new markets for food.

The new system of rotating crops, to the permanent benefit of the soil, was an important element. Another important innovation was the introduction of the humble turnip: by providing winter feed for sheep and cattle, the turnip became the most influential root grown on the farm. The area around Yetholm, as elsewhere, benefited from this and other improvements.

The adding of lime to the fields was one of the significant developments in soil improvement. This was followed by ground bone manure, introduced to Scotland in 1825. Farming became more and more of a science: the Royal Highland and Agricultural Society, which is the oldest of its kind in Scotland, was founded in 1784 and proved to be a valuable and beneficial focus.

This book can present only a broad sketch of the development of agriculture in the Yetholm area. More detailed research would be a valuable contribution to our knowledge of the past.

Sheep dominated Yetholm's farming economy. Here, wool is being baled near the Green in Kirk Yetholm in preparation for processing.

The Enclosure Movement

The movement which led to enclosure in British farming during the 18th century was, without exaggeration, a revolution. The consequences were immense and transforming. When did enclosure reach Yetholm?

Though there are frequent references to the effects of enclosure in the local chapters of the Statistical Accounts, these are oblique in that they tend to comment on the social consequences rather than the process itself. It is possible that enclosure, which regularly involved the merging of four or five small farms into one large farm, was a gradual process over the course of several years.

A further difficulty in pinpointing this social transformation may be that in England, a scheme for enclosure usually called for the promotion of a Parliamentary bill, and the appointment of commissioners to oversee the precise division of land to tenants: the process in England had its imperfections and is said to have been sometimes unfair to the poorest and smallest tenants. In Scotland, it has been said, enclosure schemes took place under legisation previously enacted by the old Scots Parliament.[1] The Yetholm chapters of the Statistical Accounts give no hint of any attempts to halt or disrupt such schemes.

Enclosure took place in Yetholm at some point before 1797, because the Rev. William Blackie, who penned in that year the Yetholm chapter of the first Statistical Account, said that many villages in the neighbouring parishes of

---

1 Tom Steel: *Scotland's Story: A New Perspective* 1984.

Hounam, Morbottle [sic] and Linton had been razed to the ground within living memory, and many of their inhabitants had withdrawn into Town Yetholm and Kirk Yetholm. He calculated that the population of his parish had more than doubled in the course of that century.

Some of these vanished settlements are named in the standard history of Roxburghshire by Alexander Jeffrey. [2] He calls them "towns" in the old meaning of farming hamlets. For example, Jeffrey writes of "the once important town of Clifton… one of the most ancient towns of Northumbria."

Likewise, he refers to "the town of Grubet" and to "the old towns" of Hounam, Capehope, Mainside, Sharplaw and Heavyside. He mentions the town of Ormeston, on the Kale Water, because it was put to the torch during the notorious invasion by the Earl of Hertford in 1545.

In the Bowmont Valley, Jeffrey also refers to the towns of Mowe, Museles, Colruist, Esheughe, Awtonburne and Cowe. The town of Molle [Mow], he reports, once had many fair houses as well as its peel, church and graveyard. All that remains of the church and graveyard at Mowhaugh today is the line of a wall in the grass and a few flat gravestones, worn smooth by centuries of wind and weather.

In Hownam as late as the year 1750, the parish minister reported, five tenants, with large families, occupied a farm now rented by one tenant; citing another example, he said that in 1756 there had been no fewer than seven tenants, with large families, now all rented by one tenant, who employed only one shepherd. In 1775 there had been nine houses, with cottagers in them, at Mainside: one year later, or two at most, the whole of the houses had been thrown down to make way for a single farmhouse. "The farmers" the author reported "will hardly allow a single house to stand on any part of their farm, except such as are necessary for their shepherd's accommodation, that the sheep may not be disturbed by the passing of people to and from the houses."

When Mr Blackie was ordained in 1786 he made a survey of Yetholm parish population: there were 491 males and 579 females. He suggests the reason for this excess of females was that when the countryside became greatly depopulated following enclosure during the previous 30 or 40 years, single women unfit for farm work, or an old widow with one or two daughters, had taken refuge in Yetholm. These women earned their

---

[2] Alexander Jeffrey: *The History and Antiquities of Roxburghshire and Adjacent Districts* Edinburgh 1859.

livelihood by spinning: perhaps, he suggested, some of them had hoed turnips by the day, and had done field work at harvest time.

He added, however, that fit women who were employable the whole season in every kind of out-work were so scarce in proportion to the demand, that a farmer would let a cottage only if furnished with a worker.

Mr Blackie spelled out the wages that farmers paid. Workers hired by the day the previous summer (1795) got 1s a day; and men before harvest got 1s 6d a day, without victuals. During harvest time many farmers gave men 1s 6d with victuals, and none gave below 1s 4d. Women got 1s 4d and none below 1s 2d. "Some years ago, 6d was reckoned equal to victuals for a day; 8d is now thought by some the proper allowance. Labourers prefer getting their victuals to an allowance in money."

Blackie calculated that at that time about 1,170 English acres in the parish were under tillage; there was some wheat, but the greatest part was barley, oats, and turnips. Much more land could be made arable, Mr Blackie added. Everyone, from small tenants with only a few acres, up to Mr Wauchope and the Marquess of Tweeddale, was growing at least some turnips: they found a ready market in Northumberland for the crop, used as winter fodder for sheep.

There were quite a number of well-known agricultural improvers throughout the country. Perhaps the best known of these in this locality was William Dawson, who from 1759 conducted his practical experiments at Frogden in the adjacent parish of Linton. At first his ideas were regarded by local farmers as extraordinary, but in time, the spectators saw that his ideas worked, and adopted them to their profit. Dawson was experimenting with such notions as a new method of land drainage; the benefits of spreading lime on the soil; and, perhaps most significant of all, the cultivation of turnips to enable cattle and sheep to survive through the winter.

Dawson was also an advocate of drill husbandry: the creation of ridges, containing the seed deposited by a drill plough. Dawson, not without difficulty, taught workers that it was possible for one man to control the drill plough, being drawn by two horses, and make straight furrows at the same time!

Dawson died in Edinburgh in 1815, and by then was known as "the Father of Scottish Agriculture".[3]

---

[3] James Fleming Leishman: *Linton Leaves* Edinburgh 1937.

Mr Blackie reported that about 4,800 sheep were maintained in Yetholm parish in summer, not counting about 2,500 lambs. These sheep were generally the largest of the Cheviot breed, and over a period of ten years, wool grown in Yetholm parish fetched on average the best prices in the country. This was the short clothing-wool. When the shepherds applied salve to their flocks, the preferred recipe was: "40 pounds of butter (24 ounces to the pound) to 6 Scots pints of tar, with which they smear 140 sheep." This was before the practice of dipping. Salve protected from ticks.

Mr Blackie had obviously been quizzing the local farmers, for he states knowledgably: "A good many years ago, a trial was made in a neighbouring parish, farther up the Bowmont Water, of crossing with the Bakewell[4] breed; but it was found so far from being an improvement, that they sold them off as speedily as possible."

The number of black cattle in Yetholm, except cows for milk, was comparatively small. There were 39 farmers' horses, both for work and riding; and the number of farmers' and hinds' cows was 50. The day of the ox was passing, but there were still about 12 oxen being reared.

The small tenants, and those inhabitants who had no land at all, kept 76 horses. The number of their milk cows was thought to be about 64.[5]

Like other neighbouring parish ministers, Mr Blackie chided the local landowners for the lack of woodland in Yetholm. "There is very little wood, and the gentlemen seem not disposed to plant any, although there is abundance of land fit for no other use."

[4] Robert Bakewell, of Dishley, Leicestershire, was a famous pioneering stock breeder of cattle, sheep and horses.

[5] This probably included the village herd, which were housed in byres that can be found to this day at the rear of some older Yetholm houses. The herd wandered through the village every morning on their way to graze on the Haugh.

Writing Up the Parish

Seated in the manse in Kirk Yetholm, the parish minister laboured with care over his report to the superintending committee in far-off Edinburgh. The year was 1835.

The Rev. John Baird was diligently researching what sometimes seemed an interminable list of questions that had been sent to him, and indeed all Church of Scotland parish ministers, by the organisers of the New Statistical Account of Scotland. Outside his window, beyond the manse garden, he could see the glebe land that came to him as part of his church living.

Mr Baird read again the results of his research on farming, the activity which dominated the economy of Yetholm. Of the 5,700 acres that comprised the parish, he calculated that more than 2,600 acres were arable, while more than 3,000 remained in permanent sheep pasture.

Downhill from the manse, the Bowmont flowed across the broad haugh, on whose 200 acres the inhabitants of Yetholm enjoyed the privilege of cutting turf and grazing their cattle.

As one of the educated leaders of the community, the parish minister had social standing, authority and a degree of independence. His opinions carried weight, and Mr Baird was not uncritical of the landowners. In his report, he expressed regret that of the five leading landowners, only one – Mr John Brack Boyd, of Cherrytrees – was resident in the parish. Another of Mr Baird's mild complaints was the lack of tree planting locally. More trees, he suggested, would benefit Yetholm in more than one way.

"The planting of a few hundred acres, besides the beauty and ornament it would add to the parish, would greatly improve and increase the value of the remainder of the land" he wrote. Tree planting, especially in the more exposed parts of the parish, would provide shelter to the farmers' stock.

Most of Yetholm's farming was in the hands of small tenant farmers. At the most modest level, there were very small fields around the two villages, patches of ground of as little as two acres (known as the Loanings). Many of these occupiers were industrious tradesmen or day-labourers who, in their spare time, cultivated these little fields, or retained them only for the convenience of a cow's pasture. These fields were held from year to year; but so long as the occupiers were able to pay the rent, they were very rarely disturbed. Baird reported that the annual rents were from £2 to £3 10s an acre, which, considering the nature of the soil and their situation, was regarded as extremely high.

Then there were other small tenant farmers, who kept one or two horses, which were used to carry coals to other villagers, or to Jedburgh to obtain a higher price; or they drove cart-loads of lime for spreading on the fields of the bigger farmers.

The biggest farms in the parish at that period were between about 400 and 1800 acres. Some of these farms were more than one-half sheep pasture. The older cultivated lands were enclosed with hedges; the more recently enclosed lands with dry-stone walls; and the sheep pastures with a ring-fence or march-fence, that is, a dry stone dike or wall surrounding the farm.

The mode of cultivation was usually the four- or five-shift rotation. The four-shift rotation consisted of taking a crop of turnips the first year; a crop of wheat or barley, sown off with grass, the second year; a crop of hay the third year; and a crop of oats the fourth year.

In the five-shift rotation, the ground was allowed to lie in pasture the fourth year, and on the fifth it was ploughed up and sown with oats.

Fertiliser for the fields, mainly lime, was transported by the cart-load. But bone manure, brought from Berwick, had been introduced in recent years, and was used extensively.

Baird estimated that about one-third of the oats grown, and two thirds of the barley, were being exported beyond the parish. But all the wheat grown locally, and probably more, was consumed within the parish.

But in Yetholm's farming economy, crops always took second place to sheep. The sheep usually preferred for the higher ground were the Cheviot. The Leicester, or long-woolled sheep, were preferred for the lower and cultivated parts of the parish. On farms that were part arable and part hill pasture, a cross between Cheviot and Leicester did well. There were two fairs annually in Kirk Yetholm: the summer fair was for the sale of Cheviot hoggs[1], and cattle; the winter sale for ewes, wedders and cattle. Town Yetholm had one sale annually, in summer, for lambs and wool.

The only breed of cattle in the parish at that time were the short-horned or Teesdale, both for giving milk and for fattening. There was a considerable trade in buying cows in Northumberland, and these were driven for sale in the busy Edinburgh markets.

The price of good land 150 years ago in Yetholm averaged about £50 per acre, though £100 an acre had been known. Pasture land averaged £10 per acre. But at that period, owing to a fall in the price of produce, the value of land was deteriorating; pasture land had fallen by nearly one-half.

By the beginning of the 19th century the spirit of agricultural improvement was very great. Baird reckoned that in the previous thirty years or so, the acreage under tillage had more than doubled. Corn was now being exported from Yetholm. Local farms were being cultivated according to the newest methods, and in that respect Yetholm was thought to be as efficient as any other part of the country. However, Baird is critical of the landlords, who, he said, maintained a high level of rents and gave no encouragement to their tenants for the improvement of their farms.

---

[1] Yearling sheep

Yetholm Loses the Working Horse

For centuries, everything in Yetholm revolved around farming. In 1952, when the Rev. Kenneth MacFadden wrote the third and last full Statistical Account of his parish, the work horse was still in regular use on local farms. By 1986, when the Rev. Joe Brown wrote a report expressing the huge changes since then, the motor car had arrived as mass private transport, and diesel power worked the traction in nearly all farming.

Mr MacFadden in 1952 tells us that there are seven farms with a rateable value over £100 in the parish. For over two centuries, the Hay family, the Marquesses of Tweeddale, had been among the two largest local landowners. They had sold up altogether before the Second World War. By 1952 the Wauchopes, the other major family (but unlike the Hays, resident) retained only Lochtower, Duncanhaugh Mill and some individual fields.

Mr Brown's 1986 report emphasises that while in the last 30 years the tractor with its attached implements has fully replaced the horse as the "king of the farm", the full likely consequences of this transformation haven't yet been played out. He says, however, that although there are still a good number of small farms, only 17 employees still work full-time in agriculture.

MacFadden tells us that even in 1952, most young men and women were already working elsewhere, the majority for firms in Kelso. Under the wartime government, there had been pressure on local farmers to shift from the livestock farming most natural to this area to mixed farming. By 1952, this was causing deterioration in the upland sheep pastures, and the profits of beef cattle – for preference Aberdeen Angus crossed, especially with Herefords – are essential to a good living from the land.

Joe Brown reports this still to be true in 1986 but by then, the favoured crosses for the Aberdeens come from the Continent: Shorthorns have never been popular hereabouts as they demand richer grazing.

Joining the European Union has, however, also led to a great increase in cereal growing, especially of malting barley. Brown says yields have grown from 35 cwt. per acre to 50 cwt., that farmers prefer to use autumn-sown barley, and that oilseed rape has become popular.

In 1952, the Statistical Account had noted a number of other farming-related employments, grooms for the workhorses being the most obvious, although MacFadden gives no numbers. He reports, however, that one traditional blacksmith can still earn a full-time living locally though twice a week he must go to Mindrum; but without the hunting horses, there would no longer be enough money in the craft.

He identifies nine men as "rabbit catchers", able to earn seven shillings and sixpence for a pair of bunnies. While these men help out with lambing and other seasonal tasks, MacFadden seems to be implying the less respectable term "poachers", since plenty of other edibles must have been available on local land during the hard times before, during and after the War.

The census records show the largest population of any decade (1,752 all told) in 1851; the smallest in 1931; and only 30 more people (632) in 1951.

By 1986, the population is clearly growing again, but now independently of the prosperity of farming. Brown notes that by then, village houses and farm cottages are empty or (especially in the case of the latter) turned into second homes. Of the 500 residents in the parish on the electoral roll, 200 are over 65; in the two villages, 490 are eligible but 190 are retired. Eighty of the houses in the villages are occupied by single people, mostly widows. MacFadden reports 22 new family houses being built in a traditional way by the Council in Town Yetholm, the first since the War, during which only "prefabs" of different types had been provided.

He notes also that at Kirk Yetholm, many houses lack their own water supply and have to collect it by bucket from a street well. However, many of these houses are being sold to new owners, especially from Newcastle, who then install both water and electricity. Thirty-four years later, Brown notes that most houses - both owner-occupied and in public ownership – have central heating. The private (i.e. most likely the "agricultural") landlord clearly is no longer so significant.

He also reports that since 1952, 62 new Council houses have been built in Town Yetholm and 7 in Kirk Yetholm. There are 22 new private houses in Town Yetholm and 9 in Kirk Yetholm. Furthermore, since 1983, a number of tenants have used "right to buy" legislation to purchase their homes from the Council. There is little doubt that those from locally based families, and whose parents may have once worked on the land, now live in much better domestic conditions.

Yetholm's new prosperity is not, however, without paradox.

In 1986 Brown tells us that only three in ten residents were born in Scotland. He acknowledges that the community's cultural life has been much enhanced by the incomers. He regrets, however, a loss of community spirit, strong earlier in the century, because so many local families had inter-married.

The local shops and similar businesses had also been in decline. In 1952 there was a prosperous baker's shop in Kirk Yetholm and another in Town Yetholm. At that time another Kirk Yetholm firm, Messrs R. and W. Young, specialised in contract livestock movement but would also move domestic furniture when people moved home. Town Yetholm had two grocers'; a third had arrived by 1986.

In 1969 Kirk Yetholm lost its last shop. In Town Yetholm there remain just one general store, a butcher's, a garage and a post office.

In the 1980s Town Yetholm also still boasted two paper shops and a tailor-cum-gentleman's outfitter. Newspapers are no longer delivered, although the general store has a good range of them available for sale. In 2006 the Adams family sold the shop to Mr and Mrs Maltby.

The village garage, Frank Gibson's, has become a major supplier of agricultural machinery in the Borders, and the Yetholm Border Shepherds' Show, with its pre-eminence in the sheep-farming world, is still a highlight of October. What Mr R.A. Roberton of Yetholm Mains farm told the Rev. K. MacFadden over half a centuy ago is probably still true: that the Shepherds' Show is the best in the Borders because it is the latest in the season and all the sheep are in their very best condition.

The last of Yetholm's public houses, the White Swan Hotel, was always popular with workers from local farms and other drinkers. It also had accommodation; and hosted the Shepherds' Show dinner on occasion.

Yetholm Border Shepherds' Show

The first Saturday in October is a key date in the calendar of Yetholm events as it is the day of the Yetholm Border Shepherds' Show. The Show, now held on the Haugh, has been a major fixture of the Yetholm scene for over 150 years and is a showcase for a range of the local community's activities. Shepherds compete for a range of trophies by exhibiting the best examples of their flocks to the scrutiny of a judge elected from their peers. The Industrial Tent houses exhibitions and competitions for baking, preserves, flowers, vegetables, photography and the skills of the crookmaker. A sheepdog trial runs for the entire day and there is a judging class for terriers. Sporting interests are catered for with the hill race from the showfield to the top of Venchen hill and back, childrens' races and Cumberland wrestling. A recent attraction is the show and parade of vintage tractors and farm machinery.

The roots of Yetholm Border Shepherds' Show can be traced back for over 150 years to the mid-nineteenth century when the hill sheep grazings on the Cheviots were unfenced. In order to keep flocks separate from neighbouring flocks and to keep sub-flocks or hirsels on the same farm separate, the technique of hefting was developed. Hefting involves restricting a discrete sheep breeding group to a specific grazing area for all time and only using ewe lambs born to that particular group as replacement breeding ewes. Sheep so hefted have bred into them an innate knowledge of their grazing limits and remain, to all practical purposes, within them without the need for fenced boundaries. No system is wholly perfect so there would be occasions when a few would stray onto adjacent grazings. Even in the nineteenth century the Cheviot shepherds earmarked their flocks so that stock from any farm were uniquely identifiable. Each autumn shepherds identified any strangers in their respective flocks and took them to a convenient central meeting point to return them to their rightful owners and to reclaim any of their own that had strayed. Yetholm 150 years ago was more than just geographically suitable; it had in those days many more hostelries and alehouses than it has today. In 1851 there were 7 innkeepers listed in Yetholm. It is likely that, having concluded the main business of the day, the herds took the opportunity to have a rare holiday, socialise and compare the quality(or otherwise) of each other's stock and, over time, the present day schedule of sheep classes evolved. Contemporary press reports of the latter half of the 19th century and the 1845 Statistical Acount establish that regular sheep sales took place in Yetholm every September and October and may owe their origin to the exchange of strays in the first instance. In its earliest days the Show was both a show and sale. *The Scotsman* in October 1868 reports it as such giving both the prizewinners and a list of the leading prices.

Among all the agricultural shows in Scotland the Yetholm Border Shepherds' Show is the last in the agricultural show calendar, although Alwinton over the border is later by one week.

The precise inaugural date of the Show can be placed to 1854. Contemporary records indicate that, allowing for those years when the Show had to be abandoned on account of war and foot and mouth disease outbreaks, the 2004 Show would have been the 150th. At the Show dinner in 1904 the Chairman remarked that the Show had attained its half-century. The late Tibbie Herbert, who was Show Secretary from 1946 to 1979, puts the first show as taking place in the 1850's. The date of today's show is firmly fixed as the first Saturday in October but this was not always so. Earlier shows could be held almost any time in October, with a preference eventually emerging for the first or second Saturday of that month. Shows today are held on the Haugh and this appears to have been the regular venue since 1921, whereas earlier Show reports in *The Scotsman* locate it in Stenhouse Park in Town Yetholm (1913) and "a field near Yetholm" (1905). The extent to which the first shows resembled today's format is unclear but by 1929 the Minute Books of the time give a picture of an event not entirely dissimilar to recent shows. The 1926 Show had classes as follows:

Cheviot Sheep	Collie Trial	Preserves
Half-Bred Sheep	Walking Sticks	Sewing
Blackface Sheep	Turnips	Knitting
3 Part Bred sheep	Vegetables	Honey
Collie Dogs	Baking	Fancy Dress Parade
Border Terriers	Butter	

In 1927 the class for Horses in Harness was dropped, never to re-appear, and in that year there is first mention of the Fancy Dress Parade. In 1886 a "Horse Leaping" competition was introduced, incorporating a double hurdle and water jump, but it is unclear as to how long this venture into Show-Jumping lasted. The Industrial Tent which houses the non-livestock classes was a fixture of the Show by the 1920's. At that time the Show owned its own marquee. This asset appears to have been a recurrent headache for the Show Committee through its blowing down in some years, and suffering damage on a number of other occasions when it was hired out to other shows and farm sales. The presence of musical accompaniment has been a regular feature of the Show. Today, this is supplied by one of the local Pipe Bands but in earlier days the preference was for music less martial. In 1926 the Secretary (Mr Wm. Turnbull at that time) was instructed to seek three tenders for the supply of a Brass Band.

Until recently, social functions were held in association with the Show. A post-show dance used to round off the day's proceedings. An annual Show dinner for many years was a regular feature and took place either immediately after the Show or around the turn of the year. At the 1905 dinner the Chairman for the evening was Mr Rutherford from Crailing Tofts, who chose as the theme of his address Rural Depopulation (plus ca change!). The 1896 Show dinner was chaired by Colonel Wauchope, whose speech was reported in some detail by *The Scotsman*. Colonel Wauchope gave an in-depth discourse on British Foreign Policy at the time, mentioning the possibility of war with the USA, and roundly criticising the Jameson Raid. He also stated his view that Yetholm had great need of its own golf course and went on to offer to make land available for this. The dinner of 25 December 1926 had as its guest of honour the Earl of Dalkeith. Unfortunately his Lordship had to forego his supper on this particular occasion as it had to be cancelled at the last minute because of a snowstorm. In June 1985 The Hill Farming Research Organisation's Sourhope Research Station hosted a summer Barn Dance in support of Show funds.

The Yetholm Border Shepherds' Show has a regularity of occurrence the equal of any but not completely unbroken. No written record can be found prior to 1926 but it can be reasonably assumed that no show would be held between 1914 and 1919. The minute books record that the Committee took the decision to abandon the 1939 Show for the duration on account of the declaration of war on 3 Sept. that year. No minutes appear to exist between 1 March 1940 until 30 January 1946 when it was decided to resume the Show on 5 October 1946. It was at this meeting also that the late Tibbie Herbert was appointed as Secretary – a post which she filled with distinction until 1979.

The other unforseen circumstance which sometimes has led to the Show's cancellation was foot and mouth disease. The 1952 Show was cancelled for this reason and again in 2001.

As it moves into the 21st century Yetholm Show continues to enjoy sustained and enthusiastic support from both exhibitors and the wider rural community. That this is so is due in large part to the Committee's willingness to respond to changes in farming practice and to changes in interest in rural activities. When the list of classes in 1929 is compared to that of 2005 it is clear that the Show's core activities have changed little during this period but it is a fair claim that recent Shows offer a wider range of attractions and interests. For example, in 1992 Charles Grant succeeded in having the Scottish Crookmakers' Champion of Champions competition held at Yetholm Show. Individual winners from shows all over Scotland are assembled at Yetholm and an overall winner selected. The photography classes attract a year on year increase in entries. The collie dog trial attracts such a volume of entries that it has to run from the moment the showfield gate opens until it closes at the day's end. The display and cavalcade of vintage tractors can now barely be contained in the space available to them. On present performance, there is every indication that Yetholm Border Shepherds' Show will continue for the next 150 years.

An Old Man Remembers

At the 1961 Shepherds' Show a reporter interviewed Mr John Telfer, of Windywalls, Kelso, who had attended his first show in 1895.

Mr Telfer, aged 78, had been a herd at Windywalls for many years. He was now retired and had been succeeded in the job by his son, Jim.

It was as a boy of 12 years of age that Mr Telfer first attended Yetholm Show, which was then held in the top haugh, known throughout the Borders as John Stenhouse's field.

Mr Telfer saw a big difference in the show from what it was in his younger days. "In those days" Mr Telfer recalled "one could pass hours away watching the horse traps arriving at the show with their cargoes of passengers in all manner of array. It was a great sight to see all the horses waiting patiently throughout the day for the return journey, many travelling a good few miles to attend the show.

"Now the horse drawn trap is a thing of the past, and in place of the strings of horses waiting patiently one can only see serried rows of motor vehicles."[1]

---

1 *The Southern Reporter*, October 1961

Chapter 5

Sport and Leisure

High Days and Holidays

In the late 18th century the recreational habits of the Scots were few. In the vast majority of the Statistical Accounts, no amusements are recorded whatsoever.

Most of the leisure and sporting activities as we know them today probably arrived in Yetholm in the late 19th century. In their splendid book, "The Victorian and Edwardian Borderland", Peter Adamson and R. Lamont – Brown comment: "First came the Saturday half-holiday, then early closing days, and a feature of Border commercial life, the monthly holiday which often meant a trip to Edinburgh. The 1871 Bank Holiday Act led to the company holidays, first without and then with pay. As prices fell from the 1870s, more people had more money to spend on their new-found leisure."

The popular leisure activities in Yetholm in those earlier years were going to the pub for a "craic" in convivial company and a game of dominoes with other "rare souls". The card games whist and bridge were and remain popular today.

A handwritten note on Yetholm village life in the 20th century (David Hutchinson's collection) states: "At the turn of the 19/20th centuries the village had a rifle club, a curling club, and a cricket club. An attempt was made to establish a golf course at Hayhope, but it never became a success and lasted only a few years."

Old photographs suggest angling clubs existed at various times.

A billiards room was established in the present Youth Hall and Yetholm competed in a billiards league consisting of about 15 teams from both sides of the Border. The Youth Hall, formerly known as The Scout Hall, was a focus of leisure activities. Here were held meetings of the Yetholm branch of the Red Triangle Club (YMCA) of which privileges of membership were said to be a reading room, writing facilities, games room, music, bathing facilities, and refreshment.

There was a library which was transferred in 1930 to the house now occupied by Denis Young. The librarian was a Mr. Wagstaffe who had been valet to an American millionaire. It was said that many villagers borrowed books simply to hear some of "Waggie's" anecdotes !

None of these activities are to be found in Yetholm today and few records of them exist.

The Bowmontside Games and The Hand Ba' Game

In the late 19th century Yetholm was famous for the Bowmontside Games which took place on the Haugh on Fastern's Een or Shrove Tuesday, a moveable feast during February or early March.

The sports programme was part of a public holiday and was heralded by a drummer beating a drum round the two villages at 7am.

It was an athletics meeting and the games included foot races, wrestling, jumping, throwing the hammer, and putting the ball (shot). A main feature was the hill race up Venchen Hill, where the runners looped round the cottage on the hill, the Braehouse. If it was snowing, gangs of men and youths cleared a running track on the Haugh.

Yet the climax of the games was the hand ba' game; as was said at the time "the ba's the thing".

The atmosphere of the Games was captured in a letter in August 1960 to John Franklin (newspaper columnist of the Kelso Chronicle and Mail) from Andrew Patterson of Oxton who writes :

"...Yetholm was my happy hunting ground. I first competed at Yetholm 66 years ago and never missed a meeting for 10 years. During this period I won 35 first prizes at Yetholm, which did not take much winning for me, they were all scratch races and the distances suited me.

"It was a festival which attracted crowds from a wide area. There was running, jumping, pole leap, hammer throwing, putting the ball and wrestling. So you can see it was quite a programme when Fastern's Een was celebrated at Yetholm.

"The games were never put off for bad weather. I have seen four inches of snow on the ground and the committee would work hard with shovels to clear the track.

"The games started at 11am and lasted until about 2pm, then it was time for the ball game to start. Yetholm ba', however, differed from other places. In this village game you could throw, kick or smuggle the ba'! It was about three times the size of a cricket ball.

"The hails were about a mile apart, and the married men played against the single men. The game was often played in the River Bowmont."

An annual game of hand ba' is one of the oldest customs of the Borders. In Yetholm the game was played each year without fail until the outbreak of the 1914-1919 War.

For a number of years after that terrible slaughter, perhaps folk felt the contest on the Haugh would stir too painful memories of more innocent times past.

The ball was of leather and specially made for each game, usually by the local saddler or shoemaker (Mr James Turnbull at one time). It was decorated with ribbons in the Yetholm colours, yellow and light green, and donated by a leading resident.

The game was played on the Haugh, and the field of play could be quite large. A wooden post known as the "hail" (the goal) stood at each end of the playing area; one report of the game played in 1960 says one hail was at Blunty's Mill and the other at the Back Ditches. Thus the field of play on this occasion was about half a mile long. On another occasion one hail was at Hayhope and the other at Venchen.

The rules of the Yetholm game (such as they were) were said to differ from those of other Border towns in that, in Yetholm, players were allowed to kick the ball. The contest was usually between the single men of the village and the married men. The game was started by an invited guest throwing the ba' high into the air. A free-for-all then ensued, with each side trying to grab the ball, hold on to it, run and touch the hail being defended by their opponents.

Often the ball would land in the whins, and as the Bowmont flowed through the field of play, the players splashed through the river, and fell into it, as a matter of course. The game was often inconclusive because darkness intervened.

The Ba' game has occasionally been played in recent years as part of the Yetholm Festival Week in June, whereas the Bowmontside Games have not taken place since the Second World War.

The Kelso Chronicle reported the Games on Fastern's Een at Yetholm in 1927 and 1928.

In 1928, there was "brilliant weather and in consequence the villages were visited by more people than has been the case for some years... There were a fair number of competitors. The racing and wrestling were keenly contested."

"Amongst the winners were : Throwing the ball, 1 W Gladstone, Yetholm, 30ft 11in , 2 W Laidlaw, Yetholm, 30ft 7in, 3 J Stenhouse, Kirk Yetholm, 29ft 6in. Wrestling, 11st. 1 Jas Tait, Keld, 2 G Young, Kirk Yetholm, 3 Jas Martin."

"The usual ba' play followed the games, Mr D H Robertson providing the balls both for Kirk Yetholm and Town Yetholm, the former being decorated by Miss Scott and the latter by Mrs J D Turnbull. Mrs Wauchope again displayed the kindly interest she takes in the life of the villages by throwing up one of the balls."

"The following were the principal subscribers to the Games:
Mrs Wauchope of Niddrie, Major A C Marshall of Cherrytrees, Berwick Brewery Co. Ltd, Glendale Co-Operative Society, Wooler; Mrs Turnbull of The Plough Hotel in Town Yetholm; Mr A Dunn and Mr Reah of Kirk Yetholm; Messrs Watson and Douglas of Town Yetholm; Messrs A Middlemas and Son and Mr G Smith of Kelso; Dr Lauder of Morebattle; and Mr J Thorburn of Birkenhead."

"After the Games the committee and officials sat down to a sumptuous tea in The White Swan Hotel, Mr and Mrs Robson doing everything they could to attend to the wants of the company."

The Bowmontside Games are long gone, yet the foot races continued for many years at the Yetholm Border Shepherds' Show in October, the handicap races being run around the football ground. Now only the the hill race takes place around the Braehouse.

Situated in the hills, it is not surprising that Yetholm attracts the fellrunners. Yet a study of sport in the village reveals a succession of athletes over many years who became noted for their prowess and success in footraces on the track.

Best remembered today and possibly the last of the breed is one of Yetholm's most favourite sons, Bill Elliot. On Saturday, 2 January 1965, Bill Elliot won the mile handicap and the gold medal at the famous athletics meeting at Powderhall. As was stated at the time "He ran the race of his life to win the Donaldson-Best one-mile handicap prize of £80 and a gold medal." Running off a handicap of 135 yards, he won by a clear 35 yards. A total of 56 runners contested 4 heats from an original entry of 96.

Aged 22, Bill was a shepherd at Yetholm Mains and today is the shepherd at Halterburn. In the following year Bill repeated his success, a unique achievement which remains unequalled today. Running off a handicap of 80 yards, he won in a tight finish from Billy Hogarth of Morebattle. Bill's training schedule included a daily run in the hills; speed training was done around Yetholm football field and on the old railway track at Mindrum, trained by the brothers Tom and Vic Tokely.

The Tokely brothers themselves were runners of note. When not playing cricket Tom would turn out as a sprinter in distances up to 440yds, winning races at Yetholm, Morebattle, Greenlaw, Oxton, Kelso, and Peebles.

Other runners of this time were James Young, known locally as "Chop", a sprinter of great ability who should have won more races, but getting him to train was a problem. Tom says he would have matched any of the runners in his day.

George Hay ("H. George") was a distance runner and competed for many years between 1940 and 1960 winning several races, yet never the best or bigger ones.

On 12 July 1957, John Franklin, writing in the Kelso Chronicle about Fiddes Veitch who was winning races over distances of 440 and 880 yards, said "It is a long time since Yetholm produced a runner of his calibre over middle distances." At the Yetholm Sports one year, Michael Glen the Scottish mile Champion came to run the half-mile and was at the top first, yet on the way down was passed by Veitch who went on to win. What a feather in his cap that was !

Many towns and villages in the Borders had Sports Days which were always well attended and where the main features were the footraces. Although open to all, the races attracted the professional runners through sponsorship and cash prizes, which provided a useful supplement to the income of many an athlete working in the rural environment.

One was Thomas Carruthers, a journeyman tailor from Town Yetholm, who we might say is Yetholm's most famous athlete. A sprinter over short and middle distance races, flat and hurdles, over the years 1860 to 1872, he became the Scottish champion.

At the age of eighteen in 1859 in the Jedburgh Games he was first in the 100 yards, 400 yards, and 800 yards races. Similar successes followed in Games throughout the Borders until 1861 when he was persuaded to compete in a major event at Sheffield in which he was the winner. The national fame this brought meant it was time to move on to the larger stage. With family responsibilities, he was married in Town Yetholm on 20 April 1860, his earnings from athletics far exceeded those from his tailoring. In 1862 he moved to Edinburgh, which brought him into range of several major athletic events. From this time on he was a regular competitor in Sheffield, Birmingham, Manchester, Newcastle, Glasgow, Edinburgh, and London.

For the next ten years he was much sought after by promoters and nationally always near the top in the sprint races. He competed regularly in the various annual Games throughout his native Scotland. In 1869, in 22 Games he won 53 first prizes, 16 second prizes, and 3 third prizes. He must have been a phenomenal athlete to have stayed at the top over such a long period.

He possessed other talents, the most important being an inventor and maker of golf clubs, for which he became famous.

To find out more about the rich and varied life of Tom Carruthers the reader should refer to the excellent source " Golf Club Maker ", Thomas Carruthers 1840-1924, by his great-grandson, Tom Carruthers, published Cualann Press 2004.

Cricket, Football, and Tennis

Over many years these sports have been the most popular games played in Yetholm. Yet today only football is played in the village and by a team composed mainly of players who do not live in the village. The demise of these games probably reflects the age spectrum of Yetholm today, where reside few young folk with sporting interests. Few records exist of the games in bygone days, cricket being the best documented.

When cricket was first played in Yetholm remains a mystery, for the playing records can no longer be found. Yet it is known Yetholm Cricket Club was in existence in 1883. At that time there were 21 members and the subscription was 1/- yearly. The office bearers were Robert Allan, Secretary; Thos Whitelaw, Treasurer; on the Committee were Adam Cockburn, Robert Cockburn, Andrew Herbert, Thos Kennedy, John Leishman, James Luke, Thos Simpson and Robert Telfer. The Captain was Robert Allan and Wm Turnbull was the Sub Captain.

By 1886 the membership had increased to 32, but after this time interest in cricket in Yetholm declined, as it did in many other small villages. In 1890 there was no play during the summer season in Yetholm, and the attendance at the Annual General Meetings of the Club during the years 1893 to 1905 averaged no more than five. However, the Club was kept going through the efforts of its office bearers and its finances kept sound by arranging concerts and dances to raise funds. Mrs Wauchope had become Patroness and presided at the concerts.

Despite the shortage of players, cricket continued in the form of "challenges" with teams from other villages such as Morebattle, Jedburgh, Coldstream, Kelso, Milfield, Wooler, Berwick and St Boswells.

There was no play during the 1914-1919 War and the Club was reformed in 1920.

After nine years' service John Adams retired as Captain and Secretary.

Probably the definitive history of the best years of Yetholm Cricket Club was written by the sports journalist, John Franklin, in "The Border Counties Chronicle and Mail" in 1958 :

"The story of Yetholm Cricket Club uncovers many interesting tales. The oldest living member is Mr John Christie of Kirk Yetholm who is now in his 87th year. Mr Christie played his first game for the village eleven in 1886, and cricket was the summer sport of Yetholm many years before that date. The first captain he can recall was John Walker, and all games were won and lost at the Haugh. Up until 1946 cricket was played on this well known piece of ground at Yetholm until the change to the playing fields.

"Like other small village elevens, Yetholm has had its ups and downs. There was no play during both world wars, but the standard of play in between has always been high, as many clubs on both sides of the Border can readily recall.

"Some of the earliest known players were J V Adams, Robert Herbert, John Christie, W Turnbull, CA Lumsden, and AR Daw. After the first world war the Club had an outstanding team when such players as the Rev. K McFadden, a stylish bat, and the Turnbull brothers Bob and Will, brought some good victories to Yetholm Cricket Club.

"The Turnbull brothers were famed throughout the Borders for use of the long handled bat, and set up quite a few records. Angus Hume and Hugh Laidlaw were other prominent players at this period.

"The best ever bowler to play for Yetholm was the late JD Turnbull, better known to locals as 'Dixon'. Feared by all batsmen who had the pleasure to play against him, his ambition was never fulfilled. It was to take all ten wickets in the one match. He claimed nine on several occasions.

"One of the best stories connected with the bowling feats of 'Dixon' was told to me by Johnny Davidson who still plays. The scene of the story was the Pier Field, Berwick :

"A Berwick batsman took his stance and knocked a good score, and 'Dixon' was put on to bowl. Setting his field, he told Davidson to go and stand on the boundary. Watch for the third ball was his instruction. The Berwick player treated the first two with respect but they seemed really harmless. He took a chance with the third, seemingly the same, but the ball went straight into Davidson's hands. Bluff and a little "bend" on the ball were two of 'Dixon's' greatest assets. This part of the boundary is known now as 'Brown Spot'.

"Very well known as opening bats were the Tice brothers, who were as steady as a rock in breaking down the opposition bowling. Players who came into the limelight about this period were J Davidson, V Blyth, Geo. Graham, Henry Adams, J Cairns, and Geo. Young.

"After the Second World War there many new faces when the sport was again resumed. Prominent were J Tait, F Mason and J Davidson, while of the younger generation V Tokely, L Adams, and John Underwood were showing promise with bat and ball. Play was now taking place on the new playing fields, one of the loveliest village grounds in South-East Scotland.

"National Service will make a big hole in the line-up for the coming season, Geo. Tice, R Butler and H Turnbull being unavailable. The captain J Tait is an experienced player and as keen as ever, while the evergreen J Davidson, who never seems to age, will be the vice-captain. Also available for the coming season are T Tokely, GD Turnbull, G Adams, L Adams, J Young, J Butler and J Moffat, and with the inclusion of a few youngsters the Club should field a good eleven. Of the younger players Ian Law and William Robertson will soon find first team places.

"One of the Club's best friends for many years has been the President, Mr RA Robertson, much loved and respected by all, who had planted the Cricket Club Tree to commemorate the Coronation."

So wrote John Franklin in 1958, a sporting journalist and clearly a fan of Yetholm Cricket Club.

From this account it would seem that the years between the two world wars were "golden years" for cricket in Yetholm, when the team enjoyed much success. Yet Arthur Daw, the son of the aforementioned AR Daw, writing for *The Scots Magazine* in April 1978, related a story told to him by his father which "was of a match against Wooler, quite soon after 1920, in which Yetholm were dismissed for one run plus two or three extras. It seemed that Wooler had the temporary services of two Australians of near Test standard, who put the fear of death into the Yetholm team with the ferocity of their bowling. The distinction of making the one run fell to my father, not that he had much to do with it, for the ball happened to hit his bat."

Sadly we cannot trace any playing records for these times, for the scorebooks cannot be found.

"Dixon", Yetholm's finest player, served the Club well, for over 30 years he held the positions of Secretary and Treasurer. He played cricket for Yetholm for 41 years, taking hundreds of wickets, 102 in the 1933 season. A seat was erected on the ground in his memory and unveiled by the Rev. K McFadden, himself a former Yetholm cricketer who, in his address, said "Dixon" was for 30 years untiring in his efforts to promote the best interests of Yetholm Cricket Club, and it was largely to him that the Club owed its success and its very existence.

Play continued through the sixties and into the eighties with noted players such as Tom Hall, Adam Dagg, R. Hunter-Murray, J. Playfair-Hannay, R. Blacklock and others.

Again the scorebooks and minutes of the meetings cannot be found, and it is not known when cricket ceased to be played in Yetholm.

It is not known when tennis was first played in Yetholm and written records have not been found. Yet local knowledge has it that tennis was played on a grass court on the Haugh in the 1930s and 1940s. In 1948 a hard court was built at the side of the playing field. A major figure at this time was Mrs Underwood who, like "Dixon" for cricket, kept the tennis club alive through her own efforts. It is said today that she was a great fund-raiser. The club's social life was very active, dances and other functions being regular features in *The People's Journal*. There was a dance on Old Year's Night followed by a domino tournament on the afternoon of Ne'er Day, itself followed by whist and a dance.

Like the cricket, tennis in Yetholm continued to be played into the eighties. It is not known when it ended and today the courts are but relics of the past.

Football, the survivor, continues to be played on the Yetholm ground. Playing records for the early days cannot be found but recorded in the minutes of the Cricket Club dated 20 September 1923 is an application by the Football Club to use the pavilion of the Cricket Club on match days "for the convenience of the visiting clubs". This was refused by the Cricket Club, which seems surprising because the memberships of both clubs at that time were roughly the same.

The minute book of the Football Club shows it was formed on Friday, 17 August 1923 at a meeting in the Red Triangle Club in Town Yetholm. The club was named "The Cheviot Rangers", and the playing colours were green and gold.

The founding members were :
President: Rev. W L Gordon. Vice Presidents: Rev James Hogg, Dr Roger, Messrs James Kerr, John Somerville. Treasurer: Mr John White. Secretary: Mr A R Daw, and Mr James Kerr was Assistant Secretary. Captain: Mr W Wilson, and Mr Robert Wood was Vice-Captain. Committee: Messrs J Riddle, W Stenhouse, J Stenhouse, W Turnbull Jnr, Duff Carlisle, and J D Turnbull.
The Selection Committee was: W Wilson, R Wood, James Kerr, C Cranston, John Adams, Duff Carlisle, and A R Daw.

In these early years the games were played on the Haugh and not until 1935 was there a wish for change because of the nearby electric pylons. Mr Robson of Venchen was approached to provide a suitable pitch. The outcome of this request is not recorded and we can only assume that play continued on the Haugh until sport in Yetholm resumed after the Second World War on the new playing field, where the Yetholm Football Club play today.

In the beginning all matches were "friendlies" with other clubs. The Club minutes record several discussions in committee on the merit of entering competition in the Crookham and District League and in the years 1930 and 1932 the Club joined the League.

This was not a success. At a special general meeting of the Club on Wednesday, 29 March 1933, the President, Rev K MacFadden reported "the Club was in very poor financial circumstances owing to the heavy expenditure in connection with Crookham and District League". The Club withdrew from the League. The Club's finances had never been robust, membership subscription had never been more than one shilling, with a travel fee to away matches being also one shilling. The records show these fees were hard to collect. Fund raising had been essential, as with the Cricket Club, mainly through dances, concerts, and whist drives.

Play continued as before through "friendlies". In 1935 the name of the Club was changed to "Yetholm Football Club" and the colours of the playing strip were also changed to navy blue shirts with white pants and stockings.

The Club entered the Kelso and District League and the membership subscription was raised to one shilling and sixpence.

Horses have always been an important feature of the recreational scene in Yetholm. The late George Beveridge, proprietor of the Plough Hotel and the trainer of a Grand National winner, watches as one of his horses is shod in the courtyard of the Plough.

Many More Wild Flowers Then

When I came to live in Yetholm in the 1960s, people would ask "What attracted you to live here?" and I would reply: "All the lovely Mimulas". This perennial, a native of North America with bright yellow flowers, grew in masses by the Bowmont Water and by the road going over to Halterburn. Where is it now? Just a few plants here and there.

I used to carry a flower book, trying to learn the names of the flowers, many of which are not there now; those that have survived are fewer in number.

On the first day of July 1984, sitting near the Sawmill, I could see Meadow Buttercup, Daisy, Birdsfoot Trefoil, Speedwell, Red Clover, Sorrel, White Clover, Vetch, Stitchwort, Yarrow, Cinquefoil, Hawkbit and Medick. There were a further 37 flowering plants nearby and I made a list of them.

Since then fertiliser has been used on the Haugh and it is no longer a meadow. So on 4th August 2005 I went to the same spot to see what was visible from one position. Not much. So I walked around a bit and observed Buttercup, Daisy, White Clover, and small flowered Cranesbill (which does not appear on any of my earlier records).

Some days later I did a count, walking the length and breadth of the Haugh on the Town Yetholm side. I found 17 different species, but in much fewer numbers than twenty years earlier. For instance, I noticed only one Daisy and two Buttercups. Shepherd's Purse, Chickweed and Pineapple Mayweed appeared only near the electricity sub-station beside the bridge. Thyme used to grow on the Haugh. At the attractive pool by the Willow trees, people used to come with their children to picnic on the grass, while the youngsters bathed in the pool. Now the area is nettles and animal manure.

I must mention the Alkanet with its brilliant blue flowers, and the remains of a solitary Tansy plant which has only just survived the Council's roadside grass cutting.

Fewer flowering plants lead to fewer butterflies, moths and other insects, and as a consequence there are fewer birds, due to modern methods of farming.

So Many Changes in Bird Life

Soon after I came to live in Yetholm forty years ago, a friend advised me to write down the birds I saw, "because many are going to disappear." Some have; and many more species have become fewer.

For instance, there were plenty of Reed Buntings by the river in those days; now they have all gone. Then there were flocks of Linnets; now just a few. I have not seen a Redshank here for a long time. Common Gulls are no longer with us, though other Gull species are here in about the same numbers as they were.

I used to be awakened in the morning by the singing of many Swallows. Now you are lucky to hear one at a time, and the telephone wires are no longer crowded by hundreds of them. The year 1991 was a bad one for Housemartins; in fact, the only ones I saw that year were two in Bamburgh! They have come back, but not so many as before. Where I have counted their nests, these are down to one-third. Swifts used to fly around in flocks in the evening screaming their songs, and I do miss that sound. I heard four doing this once last year (2005).

During the Second World War, when I had a bout of flu in Glasgow, I cheered myself up by imagining I was lying in a hayfield with a Skylark singing overhead. Not much chance now! Skylarks have had to move into the hills because the earlier sown crops have grown too high by the time they are nesting. Lapwings have the same problem. There must have been a lot more larks hundreds of years ago, when our ancestors made pies of larks' tongues!

During the recent foot and mouth epidemic in 2001, the Dippers completely disappeared from the Bowmont, but they have gradually returned.

Years ago, when the Rooks were leaving their roost in the early morning, they passed my bedroom window – hundreds of them. They kept on passing for half an hour; they could do that in minutes now. It used to be said that if you saw several "Crows" they must be Rooks, and if you saw one it must be a Crow. This no longer applies; there are far more Crows about.

Magpies have arrived in the last few years, and Collared Doves have reached us from Russia.

In the old days, as you drove along the road, flocks of mixed Finches would fly out of the hedges and then land again, further along. Now you can drive for miles without seeing one. The "little-bit-of-bread-and-no-cheese" song of the Yellowhammer is still heard occasionally. There used to be more Barn Owls.

When I came to Yetholm there were no Swans on Romany Marsh; now they breed here every year, but it means fewer Ducks, Coots and Moorhens being able to raise families.

The Cuckoo and the Green Woodpecker did not return after the trees near the War Memorial were cut down, but when the replacement trees were young a Grasshopper Warbler made its presence known. The Green Woodpecker has come back since.

The radiation from the Chernobyl explosion had a disastrous effect on the Redwings and Fieldfares, which were breeding in Scandinavia, and they don't seem to have come back here in anything like their previous numbers.

The numbers of House Sparrows and Starlings have crashed all over Britain. In the evenings great clouds of Starlings going to roost in the warmth of our towns used to be quite spectacular. There were no Sparrows for a while, but now there are groups of them, just hanging on precariously. There are none in the big towns and no one is sure why: possibly it is the effect of fumes from different chemicals in unleaded petrol. I saw two Tree Sparrows a year or so ago.

In Yetholm we were visited by three Shell Ducks in the summer of 2005. I didn't know they ever came so far inland.

Last but not least: the Kingfisher. A pair, or pairs of their descendants, have been in the Yetholm area ever since I came here. Dr Wickham has a good story about an encounter between a Kingfisher and a Sparrowhawk. Sparrowhawks are much more numerous than they used to be and they frequent gardens more often.

Lack of nesting places in trees, hedges and on the ground have contributed to the loss of birds, as well as lack of the insects needed to feed the young, even of seed-eating birds. As with the wild flowers, modern farming methods have been the cause, but there are encouraging signs of an improvement now, for example, not planting crops right up to the field edges.

Hill-walking in the Cheviots

That the Cheviot Hills around Yetholm (and indeed as a whole) are quiet, virtually uninhabited areas is largely due to their rounded un-mountainous appearance. The creation of two major walks – the Pennine Way and St Cuthbert's Way – has certainly added to the number of people to be found in the hills, but once off these paths the hills retain their secretive, intimate nature. The towering crags and pinnacled heights of the Lake District and the Highlands are absent here, save for a few hidden outcrops such as the Henhole and the Bizzle on the flanks of Cheviot.

The hillsides above the narrow, deeply incised valleys do tend to be steep – but only for short distances – and rarely does the angle exceed 50 degrees. It is with relative ease that walkers can climb out of one valley and into the next perhaps two or three times in a day's walk, thus enjoying a change of scenery and character not available in higher and more rugged terrain.

By the Middle Ages most of the deciduous forest covering the hills had been cleared. The sheep that took their name from the hills ensured that new growth of trees would not occur. The andesitic lavas provided for the most part good nutrients for the sheep's fescue and other grasses, so that flocks could flourish and the landowners with them. Where rhyolitic andesites appear, such as in the Heatherhope area south-east of Hownam, the more acidic soils are reflected in the greater areas of heather – there, too, put to good use by farmers as grouse moors.

The sheep control the plant-life of the hills. For the non-expert, however, a variety of low-growing hill plants can be found – mostly heath bedstraw, tormentil, and thyme, with cloudberry evident on the higher ridges and plateaux. Occasional patches of violets, wild pansies and birdsfoot trefoil are seen. Bushy patches of greater woodrush leaves appear as a remnant of one-time forest-floor cover. Saxifrages can be found in the rocky crevices of the various cleuchs and in the late summer the walker may come across banks of bilberries if the sheep haven't got there first.

There tends to be a paucity of bird life on these bare hills. Larks, meadow pipits, wheatear and stonechats are fairly common and of course the moorland birds – the grouse, the curlew, an occasional golden plover and now an even rarer ring-ouzel. Dippers are evident by the streams, and in the lower valley, lapwings decreasingly so. Ravens can be heard above the crags in the Henhole and the remoter cleuchs, and buzzards are common.

Badgers, foxes and rabbits are the most likely mammals to be seen on the hills and deer on the lower ground, or where there happens to be tree cover.

Some names the map-reading walker will come across may need explanation:

A bield or stell, shelters for sheep, are Norse words in origin, the latter name being most common.

Near Hownam is Buchtrig Farm. Bught comes from the Norse for a shed but refers to a small sheepfold.

Cleugh or cleuch (Norse) is a steep sided valley or cleft.

Haugh (Anglo-Saxon) is the flat land beside a river.

Hope is a sheltered valley or flat area.

Kaim (Norse) is a round hilltop

Knowe (Anglo-Saxon) is a small rounded hill, usually a spur from a higher hill: also kip.

Law: a bold hill

Linn/spout: a waterfall

Shaw: a wood

Shiel: upper summer grazings

Sike: a ditch or straight water course

Toft: a homestead

The lairds of Yetholm, the Wauchopes, have a name meaning a warm [i.e. mild] valley.

The Pennine Way

The Pennine Way was dreamed up by the campaigning access journalist, Tom Stevenson in 1935, after two American girls, coming to England on a walking holiday, had written to him asking if Britain had anything similar to the 2,000-mile Appalachian Trail, which runs from Maine to Georgia.

In a ground-breaking article in the *Daily Herald* on 22 June, Stevenson proposed "a long green trail" from the Peak to the Cheviots. This need be no "concrete or asphalt track", he said, "just a faint line on the Ordnance Map, which the feet of grateful pilgrims would, with the passing years, engrave on the face of the land."

It was to take another 30 years of campaigning for Tom's dream to become a reality. It was officially inaugurated at a ceremony at Malham Farm on 24 April, 1965, and that "faint line" became probably the best known and most heavily used footpath in Britain.

In the autumn of 1968 Tom Stevenson retired as secretary of the Ramblers' Association, whose members had been heavily involved in the establishing of the Pennine Way, and the occasion was marked by a dinner at the National Liberal Club in the following February. The speaker was the late Barbara Castle, M.P. who had been a member of the early working parties on the proposed line of the Pennine Way, and Lord Strong, chairman of the National Parks Commission at the time of its official opening.

A review in the *Manchester Guardian* on Saturday, 2 July 2001 noted that the "latest figures show that over 250,000 walkers a year set off from Edale to attempt this classic route up the backbone of England to Kirk Yetholm across the Scottish Border."

The route enters or passes through all the northern counties of England, half its distance lies within the boundaries of Yorkshire, about a third is in Northumbria, and the other counties are visited briefly. Three National Parks (The Peak District, the Yorkshire Dales and Northumberland) and a Nature Reserve (Moor House) are linked by the route, as is part of the English/ Scottish border fence.

Among the 1965 signatories in the visitors' book at the Plough Hotel were three MP's: Barbara Castle, Hugh Dalton and Geoffrey de Freitas.

St. Cuthbert's Way

The life and progress of Saint Cuthbert has provided the inspiration for the route which passes through Yetholm and Kirk Yetholm. It was opened in the summer of 1996 and leads from Melrose, where St. Cuthbert is said to have started his ministry, to Holy Island (Lindisfarne) where he ended his days. He travelled widely, visiting people in remote parts of the area and must have known the Border country very well.

The full distance of the walk is 62 miles (100 km). From Melrose the route passes through the Eildon Hills to Bowden and then via Newtown St. Boswells to reach the Tweed. A very beautiful riverside walk is then followed to Maxton. Dere Street is picked up and followed over Lilliardsedge to Harestanes.

The route continues past the imposing ruin of Cessford Castle to Morebattle, Town Yetholm and Kirk Yetholm. The Pennine Way is then followed out of Kirk Yetholm for a short distance, before it is left to cross the Border fence below Eccles Cairn to enter the Northumberland National Park. The route carries on through Elsdonburn and Hethpool to reach the busy market town of Wooler.

Weetwood Moor is then crossed before the route reaches St. Cuthbert's Cave. This is a large sandstone outcrop where the saint's body is said to have rested the first night after leaving Holy Island in A.D.875 when Vikings forced the monks to flee. The walk passes through woodland at Kyloe before reaching Fenwick and then embarking on the crossing to Lindisfarne with its superb priory and castle. The route of St. Cuthbert's Way leading from Melrose to

Holy Island thus links a number of places associated with his story and can be enjoyed as a modern-day pilgrimage.

The driving force behind the creation of St Cuthbert's Way was Roger Smith, who held the post of walking development officer within Scottish Borders Enterprise. He was the individual who made it a reality, and he did so by obtaining all the necessary permissions from farmers and other landowners within the space of 18 months.[1]

---

[1] Roger Smith and Ron Shaw. *St Cuthbert's Way: Official Trail Guide* 1997.

The E2 Europath

The British sections of the E2 European long distance footpath were formally opened at a ceremony in Kirk Yetholm in September 1999. Kirk Yetholm was chosen both for its symbolic closeness to the England-Scotland border and for its strategic importance as a footpath link between the Pennine Way and St. Cuthbert's Way, which takes the E2 onwards to Melrose. From there the route follows the Southern Upland Way to Stranraer, on the west coast of Scotland, which in turn provides a ferry link with Northern Ireland.

Tom Stevenson, back in 1935, in choosing Kirk Yetholm as the finishing point of the Pennine Way, could never have imagined that Kirk Yetholm and the Pennine Way would become a vital link in a new European long distance footpath from Stranraer to Nice!

A further link is now being actively developed, which will take the route from Peebles across the Clyde to join the Clyde Walkway to Glasgow and then via the West Highland Way and the Great Glen Way to Inverness, capital of the Highlands. Thus there will also be a footpath link from Kirk Yetholm to Inverness.[1]

---

[1] *The Great Outdoor Magazine* December 1999

The Spittal Trip

A regular feature of village life was an annual trip to the seaside: in Yetholm this was to Spittal Promenade at the mouth of the Tweed at Berwick. The origin of the event is not known, but perhaps like a similar trip to Spittal from Kelso, it was first organised by the Kirk to allow children to sample the sea air. In the early years the children and adults were transported by horse and cart to Mindrum railway station, from where they travelled to Tweedmouth Station by train. In later years the transport was by charabanc. The annual Spittal Trip features in village life today and is organised by the ladies of the village.

In the early years of the annual Spittal Trip, the adults and children were conveyed by as many as 20 decorated carts to Mindrum railway station, and thence by train to the coast. It was a holiday for the whole village. This photograph was taken in 1913.

Happy Days

This poem, recalling happy childhood days in Yetholm, was composed by the late Edith Spence. Edith, who was originally from Newcastle, was an assistant in Hardie's general store, and gave a copy of the poem to her colleague and friend, Bessie Martin. Edith died in 1995, aged 86.

How oft in days that were we strayed
With joy in many a Border glade
On russet carpets wet with dew
We watched the latticed sun come through
The tall green trees.

And woodland flowers all sparkling bright
Turned thankful faces towards the light
The lark then mounting o'er the earth
Poured forth his song of golden worth
And tho' we saw him not - we heard
And thanked God for this lovely bird.

And so on paths of verdant green
We left behind the busy scene
And strode on hills 'neath which were laid
Those bygone warriors of the plaid
All sleeping now their dreamless sleep
In pastured beauty profound and deep.

Chapter 6

The Churches' Influence

A Choice of Pulpits

What role has the Presbyterian church played in the Yetholm story? Who were the individuals who tended the spiritual welfare of the village? There have been several different pulpits in Yetholm during the past 200 years, and we have the names of a number of the occupants. The reasons underlying the succession of presbyterian denominations in the village is a tangled story. But first it may help if we slot a few names into the social context in which they were working.

Halfway through the 19th century, Yetholm was still relatively isolated. We can try to travel back there, by imagining if we can what everyday life at that time must have been like.

There was no radio, no television, no cinema. There were few newspapers or magazines, and only a limited library of relatively expensive books. Consequently, rural communities such as Yetholm were close-knit, and much less open to outside influences than they are today. Life in the village was geared to the pace of a farming economy, which was the pace of the horse and cart, and the steady progression of the four seasons. For the farm worker, solitude was the norm. This solitude while at work in the fields doubtless encouraged reflection and introspective thought. Perhaps it was easier to see the hand of God at work when one was working amid Nature in the countryside.

Religion, as represented by the local church, inevitably played a much more prominent role in society than it does today. For many villagers, the Bible and its teaching had much greater influence on their lives. The minister, along with the schoolmaster and the local landowner, was an influential leader of the community.

Virtually everyone attended church on Sunday, many of them walking long distances. The Sabbath church service might last three hours or more.

In Isa Nichol's lifetime there were three churches in Yetholm – the Church of Scotland; the Free Church (at the summit of Dow Brae); and the United Presbyterian Church (now the Wauchope Hall). As Isa wrote in her memoir: "All three churches were faithfully attended. People walked over the hills for miles, or came in carts. Shepherds even bringing their dogs."

Church meetings, even for reluctant attenders, answered a need in individuals who were by nature gregarious. For some at least, the discussion of spiritual questions, holding out hope of a better life in the next world, would be a comfort, providing solace in an often hard world.

For the parish minister, and perhaps for the appointed elders of the congregation also, their religious belief was the dominant factor in their daily lives.

After the Reformation

It is a mistake to see the Reformation in Scotland in the 16th century as a sudden event, arriving with John Knox from the continent of Europe about 1560. It is a further error to think that Knox's oratory and writings during his lifetime swiftly made the presbyterian Church of Scotland a secure and permanent institution.

The historical fact is that after the death of Knox, religious tumult continued throughout Scotland for more than one hundred years. This was a passionate, life-or-death struggle, regularly involving the power of the monarchy itself, as a bitter ideological war between presbyterianism and episcopacy swayed, now one way, now the other. A lot of blood was spilled, by both sides.

Only with the Revolution of 1688, when James II fled the country to be replaced by William of Orange, was a presbyterian form of church government in Scotland permanently assured. Not that this momentous event ended all the argument: it only changed its nature.

Enter the Secesssion Church

For more than 200 years, from the Reformation until 1785, the Church of Scotland parish church in Kirk Yetholm ministered unchallenged to the spiritual needs of the village. In 1785, however, when the parish minister, the Rev. Joseph Leck, died aged 86, there was a crisis.

In accordance with the established system of patronage, the name of the new minister was proposed by the heritors, i.e. the local landowners, but the new man was not acceptable to the congregation.

At this point the Secession Church enters the Yetholm picture. In 1747 the Rev. Ebenezer Erskine, a minister of the Kirk in Stirling, and his followers had formed the Associate (Burgher) Synod, seceding from the Church of Scotland. It became known as the Secession Church.

It seceded on fundamental questions regarding the relationship between Church and State. It regarded the Church of Scotland as lax in matters of doctrine and discipline. The dissidents opposed the role of patronage in the appointment of ministers to parishes. Some challenged the lawfulness of the oath, required of burgesses in certain towns, to acknowledge the National Church established by law. They were adamant that civil magistrates had no powers in matters of religion. Another vexed question was whether the covenants of the Church were binding on posterity.

It was not long, however, before the Secession Church split in two, these sections becoming known as the Burghers and the Anti-Burghers; and in 1799 each of these two factions split once more: so there were now,

The Associate (Burgher) Meeting House,which was part of the Secession Church, stood at the top of Dow Brae, until it was replaced on the same site by St James' Free Church of Scotland about 1882. The Free Church building ceased to be used for worship in 1940, when the congregation united with the Church of Scotland.

confusingly to the uninitiated, Old Light Burghers, and New Light Burghers; and Old Light Anti-Burghers and New Light Anti-Burghers. These were referred to more conveniently as "the Auld Licht" and "the New Licht".

At its outset the Secession Church was undoubtedly responding to a popular mood, because within five years of its founding there were 46 congregations in Scotland, and when the Secessionists established themselves in Yetholm, more than half of the 1200 inhabitants were sufficiently moved to desert the Church of Scotland for the new Secession Church.

The first minister of the new congregation, who was inducted in 1787, was the Rev. Robert Shirra. who had been a member of the Associate congregation in Stirling. During the next year the dissenters built their own church, at the top of Dow Brae, with sittings for 600 people. Mr Shirra's meeting-house was usually filled, and often crowded.[1]

The Secessionists' meeting-house at Dow Brae was to continue for almost a century, before it was demolished to make way for the Free Church building, in 1882. The name of Mr Shirra's glebe land lives on in "Shirrafield", the home of Mr Harry Robson.

In 1799 the second split within the Secession Church was to have its consequence for Mr Shirra and his Yetholm congregation. The controversy rumbled on in the village for some 15 years until 1814 when, because of "a great want of harmony in the congregation", 200 members left.

---

[1] James Tait *Two Centuries of Church Life* Kelso 1889, p.156

The United Presbyterian Church

The 200 people who left the Secession Church formed a congregation of the United Presbyterian Church, constructing their own building (later to become the Wauchope Hall). The first minister was the Rev. Walter Hume. [1]

A century later, however, in 1914, the U.P. congregation united with the Free Church. Mrs Wauchope bought the redundant U.P. hall and presented it to the village, which named the building after her family.

In 1900 most congregations of the Free Church of Scotland came together with the United Presbyterian Church to become the United Free Church.

A further historic step on the path to presbyterian unity took place in 1929, when the United Free Church came together with the established Church of Scotland.

---

[1] There is a persistent legend that the former brewery at Montgomerie Place was at one time used as a church. This is given credence by one local historian, James Tait: "Two Centuries of Border Church Life" (1889) who states that while one of the newly formed congregations was awaiting completion of their new church, they met temporarily in a building belonging to Mr Robert Elliot, then a brewer in the village. It is not certain, however, whether the story refers to those who built the Secessionist Church at Dow Brae about 1788, or to those who left in 1814 to join the United Presbyterian Church and build what later became the Wauchope Hall.

Patronage: A Profound Argument

The issue of patronage was a relatively simple one; or at least it is less baffling than certain other debates of the period. We shake our heads today , wondering what impelled some presbyterian denominations, certainly in Scotland, to divide and divide again, until they became very small sects, each convinced that God had revealed to them a more pure form of the truth.

One important factor must be the nature of the Scot. There is an old saying, "Scratch a Scot and you find a philosopher." Virtually every Scot has an inherited instinct to weigh the other man's views, to challenge the opinions of his fellows. He examines any declaration, searching for a flaw. Many Scots are attracted to disputation. It was almost inevitable, then, that in the physical and intellectual isolation of rural communities in the 18th and 19th centuries, when the minister of "Congregation A" declared in all sincerity that "Congregation B" was misinterpreting the Bible, he found a receptive audience. The minister's declaration was made from the best of motives: he offered it as the pursuit of God's will.

No one today, apart from a handful of theologians, really understands what were the issues on which the Yetholm congregations decided to part company.

When one reads today the sermons written by these preachers – men who were recognised as the leading religious orators of their day – one's reaction is, on the whole, disappointment. These good men are expounding upon Biblical texts which were expressed in the language of the Authorised Version, more familiar to the subjects of King James VI in 1611. When one reads books of 19th century sermons, they do not reveal many preachers who were tackling the social issues of the day. It may be, of course, that these 19th century preachers were speaking in some sort of code that made their message quite clear to their congregation; perhaps the power of their message has been lost to us in the intervening 200 years. Language does change over the course of two centuries. However, there must be a suspicion that 200 years ago, effective pulpit orators were thin on the ground. For every Victorian preacher who from the pulpit advocated improvement of social conditions, there were scores who felt more comfortable with theology and the deeds of the Old Testament prophets.

Why was Patronage unacceptable?

There is in the archive of Yetholm History Society an anonymous and undated paper headed "The Church at Yetholm". in which the writer summarises the custom of patronage.

"Following the Patronage Act of Parliament 1711, ministers were presented to parishes by local landowners who were responsible for providing the minister's stipend and manse and for providing and maintaining the parish with a suitable church for worship."

In passing the 1711 Act, Parliament, it would seem, was taking the logical view that those who paid the minister and provided the church building and manse – the heritors – should have a decisive say in choosing the minister. Such is the accepted view in secular society: he who pays the piper calls the tune. But this was not a secular situation. It raised a spiritual issue, which is not susceptible to earthly legislation. Patronage involved doctrine, faith, and the relationship between man and God. This conflict smouldered slowly, but eventually led to the flame of Disruption in 1843.

The Disruption caused a great shock in the Church of Scotland: no fewer than 451 ministers (about 40 per cent of the total) resigned their livings and formed the Free Church of Scotland. Giving up their manse and income was a tremendous step for these men; no act could show more clearly their faith and the depth of their convictions.

The Disruption was the culmination of a contest regarding the system of patronage and related matters that had lasted for 200 years. One authority[1]

---

[1] The Rev. John Reith. See Ecclesiastical History in Francis H. Groome: *Ordnance Gazetteer of Scotland* (New Edition) Edinburgh 1901.

has pointed out that patronage, after being twice abolished by Parliament – in 1649 and 1690 – was restored by the Act of 1711. "According to this statute a presbytery was bound to ordain or induct to a vacant parish the qualified presentee of the patron, the call of the people being regarded as a mere form." The Evangelical party in the Church had always opposed this as a principle; and the Evangelicals, "having become the majority, passed in 1834 the Veto Act, according to which no minister was to be intruded on a parish contrary to the will of the people."

The controversy continued to rage, successively within the Church, in both houses of Parliament, and the Court of Session before the decisive act of protest, when 451 ministers, headed by the great Dr Thomas Chalmers, walked out of the General Assembly of the Church of Scotland when it convened in Edinburgh on 18 May 1843. Thirty years were to pass before patronage was finally abolished in 1874 by Parliament.

Four Manses

There is only one church manse in Yetholm today, but there are still four buildings in the village that once provided a home for the local minister:

The United Presbyterian manse was at the foot of the village and is now called, appropriately, The Old Manse.

The manse of the Secession Church, when the Rev. Robert Shirra was minister, is Shirrafield.

The Free Church manse was Copsewood, near the southern edge of Town Yetholm. The Free Church building at the summit of Dow Brae (St James') ceased to be used for worship in 1940, and was disposed of by the Church. The last minister to occupy this charge was the Rev. Robert H. MacAlister.

The Church of Scotland manse, which stands across the road from the church building, was built in 1788, on the site of an earlier building.

The Evangelistic Gospel Mission

There is also in the village a non-denominational church. This is the Evangelistic Gospel Mission, better known to most villagers as the Mission Hall. It was built a few years before the Second World War broke out in 1939. The Mission was run originally by a married couple named Colville who lived in one of the houses north of Dow Brae. During the War the military took over the building as accommodation. The Mission resumed its work in 1957, when it was re-opened by Mr James Stewart, a preacher from Glasgow.

Since 1999 the minister has been Mr Lars Kirkland. The Mission conducts a regular weekly programme of worship, including a religious service on Sunday, Bible study and a Bible class for children.

Chapter 7

The Schools

A Hard Row to Hoe: The Parish School

An unvarnished account of the difficulties under which Kirk Yetholm Parish School struggled each day in the 1860s to give an education to local children is set forth in a log-book on deposit in the National Archives of Scotland.[1]

The rural environment that the book describes is a world away from its urban counterparts, the key difference being the demands made by a predominantly agricultural economy upon farming families and their offspring.

Kirk Yetholm Parish School was situated in the Old Schoolhouse (now the Youth Hostel) and the events that are related in the log-book preceded the great reforming Education Act of 1872, in which a key element was the introduction of compulsory attendance.

Prior to 1872, parish schools were still regarded as an adjunct of the Church; the schoolmaster was still a vassal of the parish minister and the Presbytery. The schoolhouse was visited regularly by the parish minister, and by appointed delegates of the Presbytery of Kelso, as well as by an H.M. Inspector of Schools.

That the Scottish educational system before 1872 was failing in the objectives set originally by the Church is shown by the report of a commission of enquiry published in 1867; this report concluded that one-fifth of Scottish children of school age were not in school, and only one-half of those at school

---

[1] General Register House, Edinburgh (File CH2/671/14)

were at inspected schools. In most cases the attendance was very irregular.[2] The principal author of the handwritten log-book was the schoolmaster, Mr Robert Reid. Mr Reid is very frank in keeping his superiors informed of the periodic difficulties under which the school laboured.

October 8, 1866: "It may be noticed generally that the smallness of attendance is consequent on the lateness of the harvest in this locality. It is, of course, the rule here, as in most other country districts, that the crops (cereal) must be secured and the potatoes taken up, before the children can be sent to school."

The school had re-opened that day after the harvest vacation. "Very bad turn-out of scholars. No particular work done during the short time we were in school..."

Attendance by the scholars fluctuated wildly, depending on a number of factors. For a start, the children had to walk to school, and there are frequent entries in the log-book about bad weather, including heavy falls of snow in midwinter.

Some parents seem to have had an ambivalent attitude towards the education of their children. Undoubtedly they were under the pressures of economic circumstances; the family needed every available pair of hands. That was the immediate, short-term advantage, which had to be balanced against a more distant and sporadic ambition of a proficiency in mathematics, geography or Latin.

October 17, 1865: "Attendance very small today – the country children being detained by the wetness of the day, and several of the town children having gone to see the Kelso races."

In July 1867 Mr Reid noted that one boy had been locked out of school on account of his lateness. His parents' counter-stroke seems to have been to take the boy out of school permanently.

In January 1869 Mr Reid had two Pupil Teachers to assist him. One of these, James Ormiston, "is 16 years of age next birthday." On January 4, 1869, when the school returned after the New Year holiday, it was James who opened up the school. Later that month: "Children still continue affected by colds, sore throats, some of them dangerously so. Attendance today was exceedingly poor. Weather wet."

---

[2] Education: *Groome's Ordnance Gazetteer of Scotland* Edinburgh 1901, p1725.

This photograph of young musicians in Yetholm school playground was taken about 1930.

February 15, 1869: "Learned today that one of the scholars has fever, apparently the same trouble that carried off so many persons in neighbouring towns."

One senses that in early 1869 Mr Reid was close to despair about the average attendance.

February 16: "Attendance slightly falling off – for what reason I know not."

February 18: "A great many absent today. The reason: a Ploughing match!!"

March 4: "As this is Hiring Week in the neighbouring towns, some of the older pupils are taking advantage of it and are getting engaged. Attendance not at all what it should be, and as a consequence 'progress' is not good."

April 7: "A great many absent this afternoon, there being a sale at Shotton, which these children were, by the consent of their parents, permitted to attend!!"

April 29: "Another pupil, Frank Douglas, has left school tonight to be engaged in field work for the summer months. Attendance, though unsteady, is rather above the average for this time of year."

So Mr Reid and his two pupil teachers coped valiantly with the hindrances of weather, harvest time, wool gathering sessions, term days and family flittings. In March 1866 H.M. Inspector, in his report, struck an optimistic note on the whole: "The school is altogether in a very promising state of efficiency... but the grammar is weak. A class in Latin has been commenced. The sewing is good."

But a complete new system of education was on the way. The 1872 Education Act set up a school board in every parish and burgh in Scotland, a universal school rate, and universal compulsory attendance. The school boards managed the schools, appointed the teachers and regulated the course of instruction. Between 1872 and 1895, 980 new schoolhouses were erected, 370 old schoolhouses were enlarged or improved, and 766 teachers' houses were built. It was the dawn of the modern era.

The Private Fee-paying Schools

In 1797 there were at least three schools in Yetholm – the parish school and two or three private schools. The Rev. William Blackie, who wrote the Yetholm chapter of the first Statistical Account, estimated that the total number of scholars might be about 80. The master of the parish school was furnished with a good schoolhouse and dwelling house, and his salary was 100 merks Scots. [1]

In 1835, when the Rev. John Baird wrote the Yetholm chapter of the second Statistical Account, there were three schools – the parish school and two unendowed schools. One of these private schools was in Town Yetholm and the other in Kirk Yetholm.

Mr Baird said the parish schoolhouse, erected only two years earlier, was without exception the handsomest building of the kind in Roxburghshire. It was attended by 100 scholars. The teacher's salary was about £30 a year, but he also earned an additional £6 as clerk to the heritors. His salary was the maximum, or two chalders of oatmeal.

Each of the two unendowed schools was attended by between 60 and 80 scholars. Several of these children were from over the Border. The fees at all the schools, per quarter, were: for reading, 2s 6d; for reading and writing, 3s; for reading, writing, and arithmetic, 3s 6d; for Latin, Greek, practical mathematics, and geography, 10s 6d. Latin and Greek were not taught in the private schools.

---

[1] The Rev. William Blaikie, Statistical Account of Scotland, 1791-1799 p670.

The total number of scholars at all the schools in the parish was 240, of whom about 40 were from England and adjoining parishes in Scotland.

Of those children under 15 years of age, very few if any could not read and write. Above 15 years, there might be many who could not write, but few or none who could not read. Mr Blackie added that the people seemed, in general, to be alive to the benefits of education.

Mr Baird was, of course, celebrated for his interest in educating the gipsy community. "Most of the tribe are able to read, though very indifferently" he said. "They seem to be alive to the benefits of education, and speak of it as the only legacy that a poor man can leave to his children; but the migratory habits of the people prevent their children from remaining long enough at school ever to make much progress."

Mr Baird said the gipsy children were generally remarked as clever. One large family of children had been taught to read by their mother at home; and he had known a father who gave a lesson every day to his two children, in the course of their migrations. Most gipsies had again and again professed their willingness to leave their children at home throughout the year for instruction and, could they only afford it, entrust them to the care of some prudent person. Most of the gipsy children attended the Sabbath school when at home; and not only did the parents willingly send them, said Mr Baird, but even the children themselves seemed delighted to attend. In most of these children there was a spirit of emulation, and a strong desire to please those who would take the trouble to notice them. Even a few of the adults attended the Sabbath school; but many were kept back by the shame of appearing more deficient than others of their own age. [2]

Some thirty years later, in 1866, Rutherfurd[3] listed four schools in Yetholm, namely:
the Parish School, under Robert McMorran, master (average attendance 75);

General Assembly School, Kirk Yetholm: Thomas H. Tait, teacher (average attendance, 52);

A private school, Town Yetholm: Adam Hunter, teacher;

Girls' School, Town Yetholm: Miss Gardiner, teacher (average attendance, 55).

---

[2] The Rev. John Baird, New Statistical Account, Vol.III, 1845 pp 168-169.

[3] Southern Counties Register and Directory, 1866 p 159.

Until 1872, responsibility for schools in parishes lay with the heritors, but the administration of education was fundamentally changed by the Education (Scotland) Act of that year, which established school boards. So, by the time the Third Statistical Account was published in the early 1950s, education in Scotland had undergone a revolution.

In January 1952 the number of pupils on the roll of Yetholm Primary School was 64 (39 boys and 25 girls). The area from which the children were drawn was much larger than the bounds of the parish; some came from the parish of Linton and some from the farm at Shotton, on the far side of the Border. There were three teachers – the headmaster and two mistresses.

Prior to 1945 there had also been a school with a resident mistress at Mowhaugh (in the parish of Morebattle). The children who attended that school were mainly the children of outlying shepherds. In 1945 the school was closed and never re-opened and the children were transported by car to Yetholm school.

At the age of 12, children who were successful in an examination went on to Kelso High School, and those unsuccessful went to Morebattle School until the leaving age of 15. Those successful children who did not wish to go to Kelso High School went to Morebattle.

In 1947 a dining hall was built at Yetholm School, the midday meal being cooked at Morebattle and brought to Yetholm. This meal cost each child 6d per day.

Evening classes were held at the school in, for example, upholstery, joinery, needlework, and country dancing. [4]

In the 1960s the school roll rose to 100, but after that went into steady decline so that the figure was again that of 1952. At July 1983 there were 59 pupils. In 1986 there were three teachers, including the headmaster, who travelled daily from Kelso. Because of the decline in the school roll the education authority examined the viability of the school, but local opinion was very strongly in favour of the school continuing in Yetholm.[5]

---

4. The Rev. Kenneth MacFadden, Third Statistical Account, 1952 pp 351-352.

5. The Rev. Joseph Brown, Third Statistical Account, 1986 pp 366-367.

The School is Modernised

For many years Roxburghshire County Council had planned to rebuild Yetholm Primary School, but with changes in local government these plans were put to one side. In 1987, however, upgrading of the school was agreed. During the period of construction – Easter 1987 to Easter 1988 – the school was moved as an entity to Morebattle Primary School. On their return, pupils found a splendid modernised school.

The former schoolhouse had been incorporated into the extension. The building now comprised a vestibule and inner entrance hall; three classrooms with adjacent project areas; a general purpose room and pupils' toilets; a dining/assembly/gym hall with a servery and hall store attached; a head teacher's room; and a staff room.

The main contractors were Leslie R. Adams Ltd., of Yetholm, and on 20 May 1988 the new school was officially opened by Councillor T. R. Dumble, chairman of the Education Committee. The school was dedicated with prayer by the Rev. Joe Brown, and a cheque was presented to the school by Mr Alastair Turnbull, chairman of Yetholm Community Council,

Chapter 8

The Gipsies: 1898 and After

Coronation Day

The festive atmosphere which pervaded the Coronation ceremony in 1898 is well conveyed by a writer, identified only as "A.M.H.", whose report appeared in the following issue of the *Border Magazine*. It is particularly interesting because of its illuminating detail, often lacking in most other contemporary accounts..

"The roads in the neighbourhood, ever since early morning, had been black with a continuous stream of Whit-Monday sightseers – the greater number of them approaching by means of bicycles, of which there must have been several thousands…"

After confirming that the parish minister, the Rev. W. Carrick Miller, had been the prime mover in arranging the event, the writer observes: "The proceedings were curious and amusing, in spite of the feeling of mockery about them."

On a table on the dais, against the gable of the Border Hotel, the crown rested on a red velvet cushion. "There was a small enclosure of reserved seats round the dais, to which people could obtain admission by payment of a small sum; said seats, consisting of planks, were soon crowded, and neighbouring cottages, from which a good view could be obtained, were covered with men sitting astride the roofs."

The first dignitary to appear on the scene was the "Lord Mayor", in a long red fur-trimmed robe, and big brass chain of office. In other accounts this gentleman is described as the "Chancellor". He may have been Archie Watt, a Yetholm grocer.

"Then came the 'Court' or committee, 'in character', who were received with a great deal of laughter. Their clothes looked as if they had been supplied from a circus, and were of a most motley description..."

"At last the minister appeared in silk gown and trencher hat, and after the crowd, at his invitation, had sung two verses of the hundredth Psalm, to the accompaniment of the brass band from Coldstream, he opened the proceedings with prayer, and then made a short speech to welcome the gathering to Yetholm.

"A short address followed from Bailie Gibson on the history of the gipsies in Scotland, (the more sympathetic that he, like the minister, are supposed to be akin to the Romany 'chals'), which being ended, 'Rule Britannia' was played by the band, and then two heralds, in marvellous costume, read the Proclamation, sentence by sentence the one repeating it after the other ..."

The Proclamation did not go unchallenged, for after the laughter and cheering which followed the reading had subsided, Mr Miller read out a letter he had just received, signed 'William Blyth' protesting against the coronation of Prince Charlie, and claiming that as the writer's father was a son of the late Queen's brother David, Charles Faa-Blyth-Rutherford was a usurper. There was an exciting pause while the minister called upon anyone who challenged King Charlie's right, to come forward, but as no one came, the "Archbishop" was summoned with all convenient speed and the band played "Wha'll be King but Charlie".

"At this moment the King arrived, and entered the enclosure with some difficulty, for his team of six donkeys suddenly became seized with obstinacy, and refused to move. The 'Archbishop' was the village blacksmith, bareheaded, attired in his working clothes, with his sleeves rolled up. He stood waiting with the crown (a brass one, studded with big imitation stones) till the King made his way to him, when he placed it on His Majesty's head, and made a short speech in Romany of which the closing words were 'Long live King Charles!'

"The people cheered merrily, and the King, standing up in his royal robes, with the crown on his head, waved his old cap, and looked supremely happy. He then mounted his donkey chariot again, in which his Queen (with a crown on her head) had remained during the ceremony, and the grand procession was marshalled, and paraded through the village, preceded by two halberdiers..."

In an animated scene, spectators crowd round the dais at Kirk Yetholm Green during the coronation of Charles Faa Blythe on 30 May, 1898.

There were said to be 10,000 people in Yetholm on Coronation Day: this was the scene as the King processed along Main Street, Town Yetholm after the crowning.

Their Majesties held a levee at the Gipsy Palace, which was very well attended, and the day was further enlivened with a public dinner, sports, a selection of music and Highland dances from the Buccleuch Pipe and Drum Band. A grand ball in the evening closed the proceedings, which A.M.H. rightly described as memorable, adding prophetically that it was not likely that anything of the kind would be seen again.

A Deeper Significance

Why were thousands of people drawn to Yetholm that day? First of all, obviously, they came to observe an unusual spectacle: a spectacle likely to be unique in their lifetime. But there was perhaps more to the occasion than that. It was a mixture. Superficially, there was the atmosphere of a circus. But the occasion also speaks of something ancient and culturally strange, even if that passed unremarked at the time.

It is easy to scoff (as Sir George Douglas did later, in his memoirs). How many Romanies were present that day? Very few, concluded Sir George. The fact is that no one could tell. Since several thousand gadgis were attracted to the historic event, it would be surprising if Romanies were able to stay away. It may be that Sir George, looking around him that day, made the common error that all gipsies are swarthy and dark haired. This is not so: in Norway, for example, there are blond, blue-eyed gipsies.

The festive atmosphere that day overlaid something that is difficult to define, something alien to the mainstream of European culture. It is surprising that the gipsy culture survives into the 21st century at all. In the era of worldwide television, satellites in space and globalisation, there remains an elusive magic at the heart of the gipsy ethos. For about 600 years they have been a part of Europe, and yet are alien to Europe. To this day, gipsies remain aloof from the mainstream. The gipsy culture continues to intrigue, and to baffle: that is why gipsies are still persecuted in central Europe, and why Travellers are often harried in the UK. Many gipsies continue to resist efforts to assimilate them. Their culture may have been driven underground, but it endures.

Why Did They Wait 15 Years?

Charles Faa Blythe was about 70 years of age at his coronation. He succeeded his mother, Queen Esther, who had died 15 years earlier in 1883. Charles presumably was recognised by the gipsy community in general as her heir, and it is not clear why 15 years elapsed before his coronation took place.

One possible theory is that an Act of Parliament, passed in order to meet local objections to gipsy encampments, had discouraged the gipsies from organising such a high-profile event as a coronation. By 1898, however, the public view of gipsies as a vague threat, or a nuisance, seems to have receded. Gipsies had become rather romantic figures.

Charles Faa Blythe, who was to be known as King Charles II, has been described as strictly upright in all his ways. He began his working life as a farm servant, but took to the hawking trade and travelled the country for 35 years before settling down in Kirk Yetholm, residing in the Gipsy Palace.

Charles reigned for only four years and died in May 1902, aged 74. Like his mother, the King was buried in the churchyard at Yetholm. His grave is not now marked with a stone; the exact spot is not known, but is believed to be immediately to the right as one enters the main gate, and within a few feet of the boundary wall.

The Man Behind The King

There is general agreement that the famous coronation of Charles Faa Blythe on 30 May 1898 was the parish minister's idea.

One of the intriguing questions about the coronation is why it was organised at that particular time. The previous monarch, Queen Esther, had been dead for 15 years: the throne was vacant. Her son Charles, was approaching 70. There is no evidence that the gipsy community felt any compelling urge to choose a new monarch: there may have been a general feeling that times were changing; that, in an era of railways and motor cars, the old traditions were fading.

Then, in early 1898, William Carrick Miller arrived in Yetholm. As the new parish minister, he was inducted in February that year. Within weeks, a coronation committee had been formed.

Mr Carrick Miller was born in Glasgow. On entering the Church of Scotland, he was appointed assistant minister of a church in Paisley; then minister of a mission church; and then inducted to St Margaret's Church, Hawick. When he arrived at Yetholm he was 39 years of age but looked younger. It is significant, I think, that Mr Carrick Miller was described by one speaker at his induction celebrations as a young man "of energy and go"; another praised the newcomer as a man "of pluck and indomitable energy". In the course of 11 years at St Margaret's, in Hawick, he had transformed a struggling congregation of not more than 100 communicants into a congregation four times that number.

His predecessor at Yetholm, the Rev. Adam Davidson, had been in that post for 45 years.

Mr Carrick Miller was undoubtedly a man with drive, and he brought that well-intentioned drive to bear on Yetholm. Everything he said at his induction celebrations suggests dedication and infectious enthusiasm. In thinking up the coronation, what were his motives? One theory is that this good man saw the coronation as a way of promoting local tourism, to the benefit of Yetholm's economy. Mr Carrick Miller saw the gipsy coronation as an opportunity to further the holiday trade, to put Yetholm "on the map".

If the tourism theory is correct, the coronation must have surpassed all of Mr Carrick Miller's expectations: it is estimated that 10,000 people were in Yetholm that day. But not everyone approved. Sir George Douglas thought the whole affair "a spurious revival". He wrote[1] disparagingly:

"For the purpose of advertising the village as a summer resort, the proceedings were undoubtedly successful; in other respects they resembled nothing more than a Bank Holiday, tempered by speechifying and a masquerade."

There is also an intriguing suggestion that neither did the event meet with the unanimous approval of Mr Carrick Miller's colleagues in the Church of Scotland. Look carefully at the photograph of the King and his retinue, lined up for a formal portrait by a professional photographer. Now the interesting feature is that there are two versions of the same photograph. In one version Mr Carrick Miller is a member of the group; in the second version the minister has been air-brushed from the picture.

It has been suggested that someone – perhaps in the Presbytery of Kelso – objected to Mr Carrick Miller, wearing his pulpit robes, playing a role in this gipsy event; that it was unseemly for the parish minister, in his robes, to take part in an event in which a considerable number of local people dressed up, it must be said, in rather outlandish ways. In his defence, Mr Carrick Miller might have pleaded that during the coronation ceremony, he had led the congregation in prayer and the singing of a psalm.

If the story of an objection is not true, why is the minister's image eradicated in one version of the same photograph? Technically, it would have been a simple matter for the professional photographer to erase the minister's image from the original glass negative. And if you look really closely at the

---

[1] Sir George Douglas: *Diversions of a Country Gentleman* London 1902.

"doctored" version, you can see where the photographer has inked-in some long grass to replace Mr Carrick Miller. If the contentious issue was indeed raised formally in the Presbytery of Kelso, the answer to the mystery may lie in the minutes of that body.

Now you see him, now you don't. In the second version of this well-known photograph (below), the parish minister, the Rev. William Carrick Miller, has been carefully removed from the glass negative and his absence camouflaged with pen and ink. The reason, it is said, was that the Church authorities objected to his participation in the coronation ceremony.

The Puzzling Matter of the Robes

Charles Faa Blythe was impressively robed for his coronation. The origin of the robes is not known for certain, but they are believed to have been obtained for the occasion from costumiers in Glasgow.

A few years ago, the well-known photographs of the robes were taken to the Museum of Scotland in Edinburgh and shown to Miss Naomi Tarrant, who at that time was in charge of the textile collection. Miss Tarrant suggested that the robes might originally have been made for use in theatrical productions: they would have been appropriate, for example, in any of the "royal" Shakespeare plays.

At the time of the coronation in Yetholm, masques, theatricals and fancy-dress entertainments were very popular. The large department stores in Glasgow (where, remember, Mr Carrick Miller had been brought up) employed large numbers of dressmakers, and the stores may well have had specialist departments providing this type of costume for hire.

Liz Arthur, a costume and textile consultant[1] offered a detailed desciption of the King's robes. She thought the robes very romanticised with a strong Celtic revival element, particularly in the metal cloak-clasp with its central boss and interlaced decoration. The combination of long cloak, tunic or coat, with tight leggings and calf-length boots, reminded her of similar masque costumes, representing Celtic kings, worn by students and staff at Glasgow School of Art in productions around this time.

---

[1] Former Curator for Textiles, Glasgow Museums

However, she added, this outfit was different in several ways: the coat was of satin patchwork, and the decoration of the boots, together with front lacings, suggested a Polish style, which indicated that the effect sought by the designer was slightly more exotic or colourful, perhaps suggesting a medieval or Central European origin.

The cloak could be a fine natural woollen fabric or possibly a heavy cotton, with an applique leaf and scrolling stem design and a broad metallic braid edging. The lining was of glazed cotton. The silk satin patchwork coat had a similar metallic braid front edging with several rows of braid round the hem. The boots were probably of either a heavy cotton or linen with a narrower braid trimming.

Another authority on historical textiles, having studied the black and white photographs, has speculated on the colours involved in the robes. She guessed that the cloak was probably a natural cream and that the applique leaf-and-scrolling-stem design was in green, with a broad metallic braid edging. She would expect the colours in the patchwork of the tunic/coat to have been varied, with red and gold represented among others.

The Gladstone Family

Gladstone is another surname that has featured prominently in the Yetholm story. On no fewer than three occasions during the 19th century, a Gladstone, in his capacity as village blacksmith and hereditary "archbishop" to the gipsy royal line, carried out the duty of crowning the gipsy monarch.

The first recorded occasion was on 25 October 1847, when George Gladstone crowned Charles Blythe I at the Cross, Kirk Yetholm. Fourteen years later, on 12 November 1861 at the same venue, he performed the same duty at the coronation of the celebrated Queen Esther (Faa). Then, on 30 May 1898, on a dais before the Border Hotel, Kirk Yetholm, George's son, Archie, wearing traditional blacksmith's garb, placed the crown on the head of Esther's son.

The coronation of 1898 was the first for which we have photographs. Archie had made the bronze crown, which was set with imitation jewels. One of Archie's sons, George, who was wearing the costume of a halberdier for the occasion, is seen standing on the extreme right of the official group photograph. George's daughter, who became Mrs Sally Crombie, lived in Spittal, Berwick. A grandson of George the halberdier, Mr George Gladstone, lives in Warren, Michigan, U.S.A. and possesses the sword that was used in the coronation.

Mrs Carolyn Marshall, who still has a house in Yetholm, is the great grand-daughter of Archie Gladstone, the blacksmith who crowned Charles Faa Blythe in 1898. She is also the great great grand-daughter of George Gladstone, who crowned both Charles Blyth I and Queen Esther.

Archie Gladstone, Village Blacksmith

Archie Gladstone the village blacksmith passed away in 1930, more than 75 years ago, and yet most people in Yetholm recognise the name.

The reason is the Gladstone family's unique association with the gipsy community which in former times inhabited Kirk Yetholm. The association with the gipsies evidently began with Archie's father, George Gladstone, who was also a blacksmith.

It is said that George first became known to the gipsies when one night he went to the assistance of a gipsy who had been set upon by four men. In time Archie's father came to be relied upon by the gipsy community as a settler of disputes. On 25 October 1847 he crowned Charles Blyth I at the Cross on Kirk Yetholm Green, and fourteen years later, on 12 November 1861, the gipsy community called on him again to perform the same duty at the coronation of Queen Esther, again at Kirk Yetholm Cross.

His son Archie, interviewed in 1927 in old age, recalled witnessing the 1861 coronation. When Archie's father died in 1889 Archie stepped into his father's shoes as village blacksmith, and also found he had inherited the post of "archbishop" to the Romany folk. He had no coronation duty to perform immediately, for Queen Esther had died six years earlier in 1883, and the Romanies had not appointed her successor.

Archie, indeed, was not called upon by the Romanies for a further nine years, when the famous gipsy coronation of May 1898 took place. This was the coronation of Charles Faa Blythe, Queen Esther's son, and who was now to be crowned as King Charles II.

There were probably more people in Yetholm that day in May 1898 than in the history of the two villages (with the possible exception of August 1304, when King Edward I and his army camped in Kirk Yetholm on his return south from one of his terrifying Scottish campaigns).

More than one source has estimated that on 30 May 1898 there were 10,000 people in Yetholm, and contemporary photographs support that figure.

Archie, who lived on in Yetholm until 1930, gave a detailed account of that day in a newspaper interview in 1927, when he was about 80 years of age.[1] He recalled the day of coronation.

"From early morning people came pouring into the village from all directions – some came in brakes, dog carts, and pony phaetons; others rode on horse-back and on cycle, while a large number came on foot.

"I remember there was one motor car, the first, I think, that had been seen in the village. There were hundreds of push cycles, which in those days were the fastest vehicles on the road.

"Across the road leading from Town Yetholm to Kirk Yetholm were all manner of decorations … A raised dais was set against the wall of the village inn, and on this was placed an old arm-chair, which served as the throne."

The platform was decorated with flags and banners, and the parish minister started the ceremony with the singing of a psalm, followed by a prayer. Archie produced for the newspaper reporter a copy of the proclamation:

"Oyez! Oyez! Oyez! It having been found that the Royal and Ancient people of Little Egypt are in trouble and are become scattered through the Royal villages of Yetholm from their having no ruler to guide and direct their kingdom, have, with the help of the people of the villages, declared for a king, lest they should become a forgotten race.

"Having considered hereditary rights of Charles Faa Blythe, whose mother, Esther Faa Blythe, did hold sway for many years over this people, they have agreed that he shall be crowned King of the Yetholm Gypsies, with all the honours due to a prince of Royal gypsy blood. Challenge who will!"

After the proclamation, the chairman read a letter from a rival claimant to the throne, a Mr David Blythe, of Chirnside. But, said Archie, no attention was paid to that. Archie then placed the crown on Charles' head: he said the crown was of brass with imitation jewels.

In accordance with custom, Archie was dressed in his working clothes, wearing his leather apron and with sleeves rolled up to the elbow. When he crowned the monarch, Archie made a short speech in the Romany tongue, which (translated) declares:

"As the hereditary archbishop of Yetholm I hereby crown Charles Faa Blythe as King of the Yetholm Gipsies, wherever they may be, and summon all his loyal people to do him respect and homage. Long live King Charles!"

---

[1] *The People's Journal*, October 1927.

Who Wrote the Proclamation?

Who actually wrote the ringing proclamation read out by Archie Gladstone following the crowning? It is suggested that the likeliest author was Mr Carrick Miller, an articulate man and the leading organiser of the entire event.

The speech was made by Archie in the Romany tongue, and there is a photocopy of the document in Yetholm History Society's archive. Some years ago the proclamation was submitted to an expert in the Romany language at the University of London. This academic confirmed that it was indeed Romany but added that it was not exactly in pure form.

This fact provided a clue. The theory is that Mr Carrick Miller (who could not have become fluent in Romany within a few weeks of his arrival in Yetholm) had composed the ringing message in English. In consultation with Charles Faa Blythe and other Romanies, Mr Carrick Miller then committed the proclamation to paper, *phonetically*, for Archie to read out on the great day.

Edmund Bogg is Disappointed

When the writer and traveller Edmund Bogg walked into Yetholm about 1898, expecting to see gipsies on every hand, he experienced a twinge of disappointment.

"Town Yetholm, which was never a gipsy stronghold, was the halting-place, on our visit, of a tribe of these wanderers, who, with caravans and usual equipments, were encamped on the green, where some half-dozen of the younger members were performing their morning ablutions, and a couple of wire-haired puppies, together with two or three large, gaunt hounds – generally an indispensable appendage to the wanderers – were stretched on the green enjoying the warm sunlight.

"Two black-eyed and brown-skinned females, mother and daughter, were preparing dinner, whilst the chief reclined in a picturesque attitude, complacently smoking the pipe of peace..."

"As we crossed the fields to Kirk Yetholm, the charming anticipation was uppermost in our minds, that we were about to enter a stronghold of Gypsydom, where the black eyes, raven locks, and the swarthy complexions of the Bohemians predominated, and where surely we should obtain a glimpse of at least one dusky princess, and receive a greater insight into the manners and customs of this peculiar race of people. The delusive charm was dissipated on entering with respect to the racial composition of the community, yet a considerable admixture of Romany blood is to be traced in the veins of the present inhabitants." [1]

---

[1] Edmund Bogg,: *A Thousand Miles of Wandering in the Border Country* Newcastle 1898, p.212.

Interviewing the King

The features of Charles Faa Blythe, the last King of the Yetholm Gipsies, are familiar from many contemporary photographs, but the following account of a conversation with him by his own fireside is unique.

The conversation took place about 1900 when he was interviewed by a lady who was on a tour of the Border country with her husband, William, during which she kept a diary.[1]

On that day the couple had left Kelso and, despite being delayed by high winds and rain squalls, reached Town Yetholm, described as clean, with a number of good-class houses. Kirk Yetholm she found "more squalid", though picturesque and pretty. After they had lunch she went to the Gipsy Palace and found the door ajar. "So I knocked at it rather timidly and, seeing an old man sitting in his shirt sleeves by the fire, put my head in and enquired politely 'Please, are you the King?' to which the old man replied 'I suppose I am, come away in, my woman.'

"So we both went in and seated ourselves in the spotlessly clean, bright little kitchen. The Queen meantime was washing her face in an adjoining apartment, or rather a cupboard sort of place. King Charles is an attractive old man with a benevolent and rather humorous face and a certain simple dignity of manner about him. After a little general conversation, he looked

[1] The journal is dated "Sunday, 28th", and the reference to high winds and squalls of rain suggests the interview may have taken place in April 1901. An extract from the journal was given to Yetholm History Society by the late Mrs Dorinda Gray, of Galewood, Milfield.

at me with a twinkle in his eye and said, "I know what you have come to see" and proceeded to take from a drawer his crown – a gorgeous tinsel affair, of which he is evidently very proud.

King Charles II, not long before his death in 1902, is seen seated at his ease near the Packhorse Bridge, Kirk Yetholm.

"I assured him that it was himself we came to see and that he was much nicer than his crown, at which he seemed quite pleased, and the Queen, who had joined us by this time, quite agreed and declared that he was worth fifty crowns. The old man then placed the crown on Willie's head, assuring him at the same time that there was nothing nasty about it. He then led him by the hand to a small mirror and made him look at himself with the crown on. I also put on the Queen's crown, or the woman's crown, as the old man called it, and was told to take plenty of time at the mirror.

"They told us that they had numbers of visitors from all parts of the world and brought out their visitors' book, in which we indeed saw the names of people from America, Australia, France, Germany – all parts. When we had purchased a photograph of the old gentleman we took our departure and as I said goodbye, the King took my hand, held it for a long time, looked at me very earnestly and said in quite an impressive voice "God bless you, hinney, and may good luck go with you." His tone and expression gave it the solemnity of a benediction and I felt moved almost as if tears would come, and the words rang in my ears all day afterwards."

Conversation With a Gipsy

In May 1998, the Stable Gallery in Yetholm mounted an exhibition to mark the centenary of the coronation of Charles Faa Blythe, the King of the Yetholm Gipsies.

The theme of the exhibition caught the attention of the newspapers, radio and television, and as a result the exhibition attracted men and women of gipsy lineage from a very wide area, including the west of Scotland, the east of Scotland and the north of England. Many of these visitors reminisced about their older relatives, such as the grandmother who felt uncomfortable sleeping indoors; she much preferred to sleep in the family caravan in the back garden. More than one man recalled as a boy seated in the dark around a family campfire, as he listened to gipsy tales from long ago.

Talking with these visitors, it became clear that individual gipsies had widely differing attitude towards their heritage. In conversation, some played down their Romany ancestry; others were obviously proud of it. It usually depended on the individual's age; the older the person, the more they were forthcoming. It seemed that in many cases, at least two generations had to pass before the individual felt able to acknowledge his or her distinctive heritage.

The exhibition convinced the writer that there are still many true gipsies around, with their own distinctive social customs, attitudes, philosophy – but that these traits are for the most part hidden, submerged beneath the surface of modern life.

One day, very near the end of the exhibiton's run, a young, smartly dressed man came in with his wife and young daughter, who would be about five or six years old. The child was strikingly beautiful, with dark hair and dark eyes. After chatting about the theme of the exhibition, the husband remarked that the true gipsy today may be a successful businessman in a big way. He knew of one family who had decided to move to Germany. They spoke no German, and had little money. Within a fortnight of arriving they were speaking German and had earned their first money by the husband offering to asphalt a car park for a local building contractor. He never looked back.

My visitor said there are men who control large businesses, but who go off quietly now and then to socialise with fellow gipsies in the community. He said a gipsy walking down a busy street in New York can pick out another gipsy from the crowd: there is a recognisable bond between them.

A common mistake is the belief that all gipsies are dark: there are, for example, blond, blue-eyed gipsies in Norway.

It is also said that gipsies are remarkably well informed about what is happening in gipsy circles at the other end of the country. "There are two men at Appleby Fair next week who will fight" said my friend. "They are settling a grudge. Everyone knows about it."

Chapter 9

The Nineteenth Century

The Yetholm Parish Militia Club

It was a time of great change. The Royal Family's affairs, especially the alleged misconduct of the prospective Queen, whose royal husband sought a divorce, was being publicly exposed in lurid detail in the popular media. A National Lottery was in full swing, making winners fabulously rich. An insurance scheme set up to ward off one misfortune for households, had a built-in excess on any claim.

The year, however, was not 1996 but 1820; the royal husband was George IV, who was heading for a coronation from which his wife Caroline was to be excluded. The media were the newspapers, as now, and in place of television were the coloured prints. Could things like these possibly happen in our day and age, including accusations of marital impropriety in the Royal Family, aired week after week in the Press?

Among the advertisements in the Kelso Mail at that time, and alongside the announcement of a Rich Wheel (a lottery with shares to be sold throughout Scotland at Post Offices, stationers, etc.) was one stating that groups of distinguished citizens had been prevailed upon to advertise a declaration in support of the King and the Monarchy. Loyalty was to be shown by signing this declaration at the Town Hall, Kelso, and other towns in the Borders.

Today we are more accustomed to signing books of condolences, and this throws light on the need of extra support which some felt the Monarchy had at that time and is part of the background to the maintenance of a militia, and therefore relevant to my subject.

At least it was a constitutional Monarchy, as well as a Protestant one, this having been established by the "Revolution" in 1688. Both Whigs and Tories were determined to keep out any Catholicism and maintain the power of Parliament. Political power was increasingly in the hands of the people but economic power remained with the nobility, landowners, mill and ship owners and those who were able to profit from exploitation of colonial resources such as sugar and tea plantations.

With the French Revolution and the Napoleonic Wars came the threat of invasion. The British Government sought to deter threatened rebellion at home and also free the Regular Army for action abroad. The militia which had developed over centuries was therefore strengthened, and in 1797 the Scottish Militia Act authorised the conscription by ballot of a Militia of 6,000 men aged between 18 and 30. The upper age limit was extended to 45 in 1802. The period of service was apparently five years.

Earlier militias, even whole units, had usually been provided by landowners from their families and tenants. The "Glorious Revolution" having preserved the class system intact, it was to the landed gentry that command of the Militia was now entrusted, in the understanding that they had most to preserve. There was already much resentment of the army throughout Scotland (it was only fifty-one years since Culloden), and having to serve under the gentry and on behalf of the Government provoked further unrest.

The parish schoolmaster was required to draw up a list of those eligible for the ballot, which was then displayed on the door of the kirk with intimation of the days on which the Deputy Lieutenant of the County would attend to hear claims for exemption from service in the Militia.

Those persons exempt from Militia service included clergymen, schoolmasters, university professors, articled clerks, apprentices, seafarers and all those with two children born in wedlock. Anyone chosen in the ballot could provide a substitute or could pay £10 to be excused – a not inconsiderable amount for a working man at that time!

The Act of 1797 was seen by many as an attack on the workers and poorer people. There were violent disturbances in protest, especially at Tranent in 1797 and Ruthven Parish in 1803. In some areas lists were torn down from the kirk doors and parish registers were forcibly removed from the schoolmaster's house. In Selkirk, mobs from Melrose and Galashiels drove the deputies out of town, and in Jedburgh some rioters were jailed.

Eventually the law-abiding citizenry bowed to the authority of King and Parliament. The Border regiments of Dumfries, Selkirk and Roxburghshire had been combined in 1802 as the Dumfries Militia. The Militias took no active part in the wars, but had released the Regular Army for foreign duties. The Dumfries Militia were admired wherever they went for their superior discipline and exemplary conduct, and the Government for its part felt the need to maintain the Militias in the face of continued unrest after the war, although they were seldom called out for training. One such muster of about 400 men took place in June 1820.

From the *Kelso Mail*, 4th October 1821:

"CAUTION TO MILITIAMEN – We formerly stated that six men were apprehended as deserters from the Dumfries-shire, &c Militia: three of whom were a few days ago committed to the Jail of this place, for the period of twelve months, in terms of the Act of the 42nd Geo. III Cap. 91, viz: six months for having enlisted into the Regular Army since their engagement with the Militia, and six months for having absented themselves from the training of the regiment in June last. In addition to this they have to serve five years more in the Militia, and afterwards fulfil their engagements with the Regular Army. Two of the above were marched, as deserters, upwards of 400 miles. – *Dumfries Journal*."

Prior to this a ballot had to be held at the Town Hall, Kelso on 20th and 27th October 1820 to supply the deficiency in the Dumfries Regiment of Militia in respect of one substitute from the 1816 ballot, "George Lamb, who had deserted the Militia and enlisted in a Regular Regiment now lying off Gibraltar, and one Bernard Common, a Jedburgh stocking-maker, who had been banished from the County of Roxburgh by the Sheriff and was lurking in the vicinity of Wooler."

In some parishes, such ballots had prompted the formation of insurance societies, through which by regular payments over the period of a ballot, those liable might find a substitute, or receive some compensation if they decided to serve.

Owing to the generosity of the late Mr Jack Robb, formerly of Blunty's Mill, Kirk Yetholm, there is in the Scottish Borders Archive at Selkirk a copy of the minutes of the Yetholm Parish Militia Club, 1820-31. This eloquent document brings to life elements of life in this Parish through the proceedings and personal signatures, occupations and addresses of upwards of 92 Yetholm men between 18 and 45 years of age who were members of that Club almost two centuries ago. These are a valuable resource for expatriates researching their ancestry, and some are forebears of people still residing in the area of Town and Kirk Yetholm. The various occupations of these parishioners paint a picture of a self-contained world which is nevertheless deeply affected by world events.

The minute book begins: "A Meeting of Persons of the Parish of Yetholm liable for the regular Militia of Scotland held at Town Yetholm in the Schoolhouse on 18th May 1820 for the purpose of establishing a Club in order to provide funds for the procuring of Substitutes to serve in the room of such of the members of the Club as might be ballotted to serve in said Militia Force." Mr George Henderson, a merchant, was installed as "Presses" and William Henderson, teacher, as Clerk. By 25th May they had drawn up a clear set of Laws for approval at a General Meeting on the 27th when James Ainslie, Baker, was made Presses, and William Henderson was also appointed Treasurer at £1:1/- stg annually.[1] Initially there were 46 members.

It must be said that the affairs of the Club were conducted with the utmost precision, the money for distribution being calculated even down to the 55th part of a penny! It is not clear how these fractions could be paid, but they were due under the Laws of the Club.

The entry money was 10/-, with 2/- to be paid half-yearly. If a member was called up by the ballot and the Club found a substitute for him he still had to pay the "excess" of £1:10/-. The Club would pay a suitable substitute £8:1/-. Substitutes were found by intimation in both Town and Kirk Yetholm of vacancies (the Town Crier was paid a fee of 1/-.) Should a member choose to serve, or to be a substitute for another member, he would then receive the bounty of £8 less £1:10/-.

If the Treasurer found himself in possession of £10 he should "put it to interest in the Bank of Scotland in the name and for the benefit of the Club."

The Club instructed whoever was to attend the October ballot to pray the Lieutenancy not to call upon Yetholm for men but to have the missing Militiamen apprehended and compelled to fulfil their duties. The sum of 5/- was paid to the Clerk for preparing this petition, and the expenses for paper and a reasonable day's wage for whoever should travel to the ballot in Kelso were all carefully accounted for. Unfortunately His Lordship declined the prayer as far too late, and the ballot was to proceed.

---

[1] In pre-decimal currency, 4 farthings equalled 1 penny (1d); 12 pennies equalled 1 shilling (1/-); and 20 shillings equalled £1.

One of the members, John Elliot, a baker in Town Yetholm, was chosen in the ballot and at a Managers' meeting on 2nd November William Simpson, a joiner in Town Yetholm and also a member, agreed to substitute in his place. He would then receive the bounty, less the excess. Persons who were balloted and not members were not the concern of the Club and though they are listed they took no part in the proceedings.

By 27th October the following year the finances were all settled and the balance of subscriptions repaid to retiring members. One or two more meetings were held and by 26th April 1823 it was agreed the prospect of a ballot was now remote. In the event of another ballot the Secretary should keep the books open and call a meeting to reconstitute the Club. On 3rd May 1823 the balance was £26:15/9d plus a farthing which was 16/2d three farthings plus ten elevenths of a penny due to each remaining member. There is no mention of how the fractions were paid!

The next Drill, of 27 Officers and 520 Men again under the Marquis of Queensberry, was to be at Dumfries from 25th June to 22nd July 1825, and required a ballot for 5 men. A meeting was called in Yetholm and the Club was re-established with 57 men on 23rd April 1825. These meetings were generally at 8 pm which may reflect the long working day as well as the time of the evening meal. Thomas Young, a mason of Town Yetholm, and Adam Tarbit of Halterburnhead were the members balloted this time. George Moffat, a shoemaker of Yetholm and William Young, shoemaker of Kelso, were to be substitutes. They were paid 1/- on acceptance by the Club, the bounties being retained until they were approved and attested for the Militia.

On 29th October 1825 the amount due to the remaining members was 4/6d and 24 fifty-fifths of a penny each!

The Regiment seems to have virtually ceased to function after the Drill of 1825. In 1828 the Officers who had served with the Regiment since the war sold most of the mess plate among themselves for £95, a little more than its value. They could see little likelihood of the Militia being active again. The proceeds were distributed to the officers in shares proportionate to their contributions to the mess.

Another ballot was still required in March 1831 and the Yetholm Militia Club was again reconstituted. Five Yetholm names were drawn, of whom one, John Dickson, labourer of Kirk Yetholm, was not a member. From the Club, those balloted were: from Kirk Yetholm, George Wilson, merchant and James Allan, a servant; and from Town Yetholm, William Grahamslaw, farmer and

Adam Oliver, a shoemaker. All four chose to be substituted. Public intimation was made in both villages as before and the substitutes found were Adam Cockburn, labourer, for George Wilson; John Kelly, shoemaker, for James Allan; Andrew Young, labourer, for William Grahamslaw; and William Mills, servant, for Adam Oliver. All came from Town Yetholm and were paid the "enlisting money" of 1/- each. It had now come to light that other Militia Clubs were much less generous than Yetholm, and the all-important bounty was reduced to £5:10/-! The substitutes were conducted to Kelso by George Wilson and John Kerr to see them examined and sworn in.

There followed one of the most interesting episodes in the Club. On 23rd March 1831 it came to the managers' notice that Andrew Young, substitute from Kirk Yetholm, intended to go to America so soon as he received the bounty. Cited before the meeting, he was examined and in order to remove all doubts he offered to allow his bounty to remain in the hands of the Treasurer till the Regiment was embodied, as security for his appearance. This was accepted but he was to be paid 10/- when he was attested.

The Dumfries Militia underwent successive cuts until 1854, when its establishment was modified under the Militia Act of that year. The uniforms, clothing (now worn out), swords, muskets and bayonets etc. were all sent for storage at Carlisle Castle and by 1855 the only firearms of the Regiment (now known as No. 81) were six "fusils". Under the earlier Acts the Militia could be embodied when there was danger of invasion or insurrection. Now this would only apply whenever there was war with a foreign power. During the Crimean War, the Militia was raised by voluntary enlistment. The total quota for Dumfries, Roxburgh and Selkirk was 512 but it appears the muster parade was a sad sight as it was very hard to recruit. The Marquis of Queensberry, Colonel of the Regiment, had to resort to recruiting his own labourers. Training improved the troops greatly but the momentum of the Napoleonic Wars had gone.

Roads in The Borders

Today we take for granted the provision of roads which are well surfaced and well maintained, paid for out of general taxation or local rates. In 1700 it was otherwise. There had been no routes planned and built by central authority since those of the Roman legions 1,300 years earlier. Most had disappeared and such as survived had been but indifferently maintained.

Border villages were linked by natural pathways using fords to cross the rivers and their tributaries and avoiding the lower ill-drained ground by the means of upland routes. These were more easily negotiable on foot or on horseback. Goods were frequently carried on horseback or pannier, because the surfaces of such roads as existed were rough and inimical to wheeled vehicles.

Such maintenance of roads as there was in the early 18th century was the responsibility of the Justices of the Peace who, with Commissioners of Supply, could be required by government pressure to carry out repairs or to construct roads. The labour for such work was to be provided by "tenants, cottagers and labouring men", who were required by law, and unpaid, to give several days annually to work on the roads. Constables enforced compliance or extracted fines from absentees. Three ten-hour days of unwilling work were thus extracted in spring before sowing, and autumn after harvest, when government pressure demanded. Good reason then for the repairs of one season to have wholly disappeared by the next.

Bridges were a rarity and often foot bridges, such as linked the two Yetholms over the Bowmont, were flimsy, temporary timber structures which disappeared when the river flooded. Fords were accepted as the norm and often served the useful purpose of satisfying the thirst not only of the horse but of the rider.

The Rev. James Rutherford, minister at Hownam in the 1790s, gave an account of the roads in his parish, much of which would, no doubt, have been equally true of the Yetholm of his day. "There are no roads but what may be called natural roads" he wrote. "The lands being hilly, and dry, and gravelly, the roads are always good in winter and in summer except for some patches to be met with on the outskirts of the parish." His next paragraph looks forward to the new developments about to overtake the district when he alludes to the ending of the system of forced labour. "The statute of labour of the county is lately converted into money by Act of Parliament and laid on tenants and occupiers of land." In other words, the wealthy were at last going to have to pay for the upkeep and improvement of the roads, and the labouring classes were to be relieved of a burdensome duty previously imposed on them and from which they got little return. "New roads are to be made and old ones kept in good repair" he wrote. "Turnpikes are considered to be of great importance to the country." Tolls on these new highways introduced the principle that the user would pay for the upkeep. Rutherford looked forward to a new age ushered in by improved communications which was to offer advantages to all. Improvements in the wool trade would see the value of land rise, to the advantage of landlord and tenant. There would be new opportunities for labour in the establishment of new manufactories for woollen cloth. From the export of the cloth would follow reciprocal trade advantages for all.

The greatest project under discussion at the time, however, was not the roads, but a canal which was to run from Berwick, up the Tweed and Teviot to Ancrum Bridge. Kelso would thus have been linked to the sea and Yetholm would also have benefited. Rutherford saw the canals in England as "one of the great sources of the riches of that kingdom."

The canal was never built, but communications were greatly advanced to Yetholm by the building of two improved roads. Before a toll road could be made it had to be shown that the existing route was inadequate and then legislation was required. Money was borrowed by the Turnpike Trustees to finance the building of the new roads and this was to be recovered by the tolls charged for their use. The task of collecting these dues was put out to tender annually, with the renter of the tolls hoping to make a profit. Toll keepers who manned the gates were employed to collect the money and to issue tickets. Under the Kelso Turnpike Act of 1793 improvements were to be made on an ancient track from Kelso to Wooler via Yetholm. The Kelso trustees' intention, no doubt, was to bring new business to the town by offering its bridge over the Tweed as an alternative route to that established at Coldstream, for coaches travelling between London and Edinburgh.

Having crossed the river, the traveller was faced with the first toll gate at Maxwellheugh before the south-eastward climb. The new road did not, however, enter either of the Yetholm villages, but veered off, by the smithy which stood where Catch-a-Penny[1] cottage stands today, and went via Cherrytrees, to the new toll house established at Old Venchen within a few yards of the national boundary and Northumberland. Town Yetholm was accessible from the junction below the Virtue Well and over the Stank. Traffic was not likely to be welcome in villages – especially when it often consisted of herds of animals.

We can almost be certain that the quarry behind the Venchen Cottages was the source of the road metal for the creation and repair of the new roads, and that the houses must also have been built for the labourers who were required.

The second turnpike road was established before 1820 to improve the route from Jedburgh to Wooler. There was a toll house on the section from Eckford and Morebattle on the Yetholm parish boundary at Primside. From there the road went on directly to Kirk Yetholm after crossing the haugh and fording the Bowmont Water before making its way up the Kirk Brae into the village. The line of this road is still clearly visible to this day behind the War Memorial. Its continuation on the further bank via the Back Ditches is now a farm track, lined in part by great oaks, which leads directly to the gates of the new cemetery above Duncanhaugh. There was no road bridge to join the two villages until the 1830s and thus no advantage before its construction in going through Town Yetholm when the new turnpike road was opened.

From Kirk Yetholm the road continued to Kirk Yetholm Mains Farm, and a new toll house, and then to the border at Shotton Burn. Apparently this turnpike road, ironically officially named "The Great Road", was not sufficiently used and by 1870 the two toll houses were closed. Kirk Yetholm Mains turnpike was abandoned, and the toll house at Primside was turned over to a gamekeeper and his large family.

---

[1] All 19th century maps show a "smithy" on this site and not a toll. Census returns from 1841 name the building as "Clock Mill Smithy". "Clock" may well be a corruption of "cleuch" – a ravine – which would certainly apply to the geography.

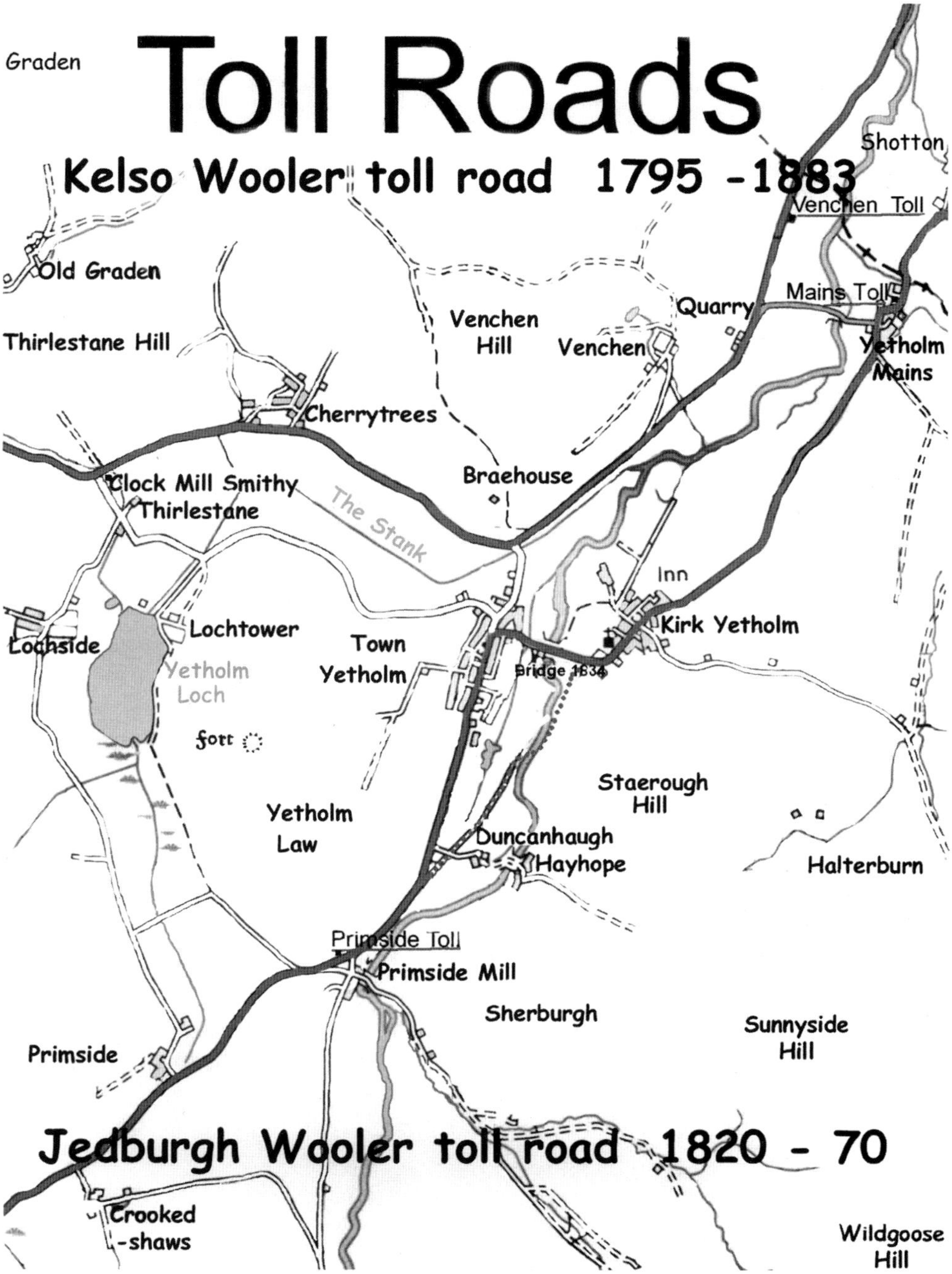
Toll Roads
Kelso Wooler toll road 1795 -1883
Graden
Shotton
Venchen Toll
Old Graden
Mains Toll
Venchen Hill
Quarry
Thirlestane Hill
Venchen
Yetholm Mains
Cherrytrees
Braehouse
Clock Mill Smithy
Thirlestane
The Stank
Inn
Lochtower
Kirk Yetholm
Lochside
Town Yetholm
Yetholm Loch
Bridge 1834
fort
Staerough Hill
Yetholm Law
Duncanhaugh
Hayhope
Halterburn
Primside Toll
Primside Mill
Sherburgh
Sunnyside Hill
Primside
Jedburgh Wooler toll road 1820 - 70
Crooked -shaws
Wildgoose Hill

Gates controlling the traffic at the tolls were spiked or "piked" on top – hence the designation "turnpike". People on foot did not have to pay to use these roads but wheeled traffic such as carts and carriages did, and the price varied according to the number of pulling animals. Riders on horseback paid less, and led horses paid a lower rate again. Cattle were charged by the score. Calves, sheep, lambs and hoggs paid also by the score but only at a quarter of the rate for cattle.

In 1834 the *Kelso Chronicle* reported the dramatic news that it was now possible "for passengers 60 miles from Edinburgh to leave home and return home the same evening, with six hours in the city to transact business." However, that meant being at Hownam's Inn at Coldstream by 4.30 a.m. to join the Red Rover coach from London and getting back to Coldstream at 9 p.m. Alternatively, you could enjoy the entire trip from Edinburgh "direct to London in 45 hours certain"!

Users of the new roads as reported in the 1840s were often the lesser tenants in Yetholm, who kept one or two horses and used their carts for the carriage of coal from Northumberland to the village, or even as far as Jedburgh. Another source of income was the bringing of lime as an agricultural fertiliser for the wealthier local farmers and also for their own use. A heavy traffic in driven herds of cattle from Northumberland to the Edinburgh markets is reported at the same period. Despite the original aspirations of the Kelso turnpike builders, the new road did not attract the public coach services running between the larger cities. The village was still dependent on the local private carriers who ran between Yetholm and Kelso for five days a week, and even less frequently to Berwick or Coldstream.

The Venchen toll continued to operate until the whole turnpike system was ended by the Roads and Bridges Act of 1883. Census returns show that Isabella Dodds, a labourer's widow, ran the toll at Primside for more than 20 years and brought up a family of three boys and one girl. Yetholm Mains toll was being run in the 1850s by another widow, with two sons and two daughters. Matilda Service at the Venchen toll in 1871 was an unmarried woman of 32 with two one-year-old children [of either sex?], but whose 12-year-old nephew, also resident, was also denoted "toll keeper". In 1881 she had been replaced by Elizabeth Nuncio, with three daughters and three sons, the oldest of whom at 16 was, like his mother, designated "toll keeper".

Surprisingly, Catch-a-Penny appears never to have been a toll. It is recorded in census returns as the Clock Mill Smithy, and was run for more than 30 years in mid-century by a John Bennet, who had as many as four employees

These photographs are a reconstruction by Brian Ashby of what the toll houses at Primside and Venchen probably looked like in the days of the turnpike roads.

to assist him. It must have served as a useful way station for the horse traffic on the turnpike road. Before him, in 1834, a Thomas Scott was the blacksmith.

What undoubtedly was of the greatest benefit to the two Yetholm villages was the completion in 1834 of the road bridge over the Bowmont and the provision of a causeway across the haugh. No longer were floods the frequent barrier they once had been. The Rev. John Baird, minister at Kirk Yetholm, records: "A very neat bridge... across the Bowmont between the villages of Town and Kirk Yetholm, is one of the greatest improvements that have taken place in the parish for many years."[2]

Of the three toll houses, two remain: Old Venchen was still occupied by the Anderson family in mid-20th century, and is, at the time of print, being altered as a large modern house. Yetholm Mains has been improved, and is still occupied. Primside toll house has disappeared completely, although it was still standing as a deserted ruin in the 1950s.

The new wealth which was to be made available through improved communications, foreseen by the Rev. Rutherford, did eventually arrive.

But it was the creation of the railways in the 1850s, and not the proposed canal, which dominated the transport system and which reduced the roads to a secondary role for most of the next hundred years. For the folk of Yetholm, Mindrum was a nearer alternative point of access to the national rail network than Kelso, and both were available by the established turnpike road.

Nevertheless, the relatively modest improvements of the 19th century roads did bring in a period of industrialisation to Yetholm. The building of the extended Blunty's Mill in the 1840s made use of the newly invented automatic looms and water-powered spinning machines, to produce blankets and other woollen textiles – a trade which only ended well after the First World War, for which military khaki had been produced. On the other hand, farmers, tenants, and employees and their families, all were able to take advantage of the widely extended market and the greater range of goods generally available through the better means of communication.

---

[2] The bridge over the Bowmont was designed and built to the plans of John Smith of Darnick, who was responsible for not only many bridges in the Border region but also a large number of mansions, which were at that time under construction or reconstruction, such as Abbotsford. Smith also designed and built a large number of churches, and in 1835 submitted a plan for Yetholm Kirk with an estimate of £1,500.

For the great advance in road building used on the toll we must thank John Macadam, who invented the modern method of road constrruction. This did not rely on the Roman system of building up from a solid foundation of large rocks followed by lesser stones until the surface layer was reached. Macadam believed that a shallow foundation, of a foot in depth, of broken stone floating upon the subsoil, was all that was required if this were topped with broken rocks no greater than one inch in size. The weight of the metal-tyred wheels of carts was then adequate to grind and compact the surface and render it waterproof. Not only were these roads cheaper to make but also were found to have the benefit of absorbing the shock on the legs of draught animals so that their working lives were often more than doubled, to seven years.

The greater revolution in transport came with the arrival of the motor vehicle in the 20th century and its ready availability through methods of mass production. It was then that the roads recovered from being eclipsed by the railways. Motor traffic was to be the greatest boost to road building, and to the improved methods of construction from which we all benefit today. However, the new pneumatic tyre had the unfortunate tendency to create a vacuum which sucked out the smaller elements of the Macadam road surface, creating clouds of dust behind the early motor vehicles, as well as destroying the waterproofing. Coal tar, a by-product of gas production, and only recently readily available, solved both of these problems.

In the late 1800s, only the wealthy merchants and gentry in the towns, or the landed aristocracy, were able to afford the upkeep of the family coach. One hundred years later the possibility of a family car was available to nearly all, resulting in the streets of Yetholm being lined with parked vehicles as it is today.

The payment for the building of roads from a local tax based on the value of property, set a precedent for the financing and organising of local services, which eventually developed and extended to cover the provision of such things as education, the police, housing, water and sewerage. Thus were we set on that new road to the complex and more accessible world in which we all now live.

A Footpath Dispute

The footpath alongside the former lade between Yetholm Mill and the Youth Hostel has been the subject of complaints for at least one hundred years. We know this from the minutes of Yetholm Parish Council.

In July 1897, for example, members of the Parish Council made clear to the District Committee in Kelso that there was to be no interference with this right-of-way. In December 1897, one of the members, Mr Watt, gave notice of his intention to ask the Parish Council to repair the footpath: he estimated the cost of this at 30 shillings, which he proposed should be found by levying a special rate. Apparently this did not come about.

The footpath was in the news again in March 1908: a local man evidently had been driving his cattle along it, and he was asked by the Parish Council to desist. Three years later, however, the Council was told of a manure heap near the dam at Kirk Yetholm; and (more serious) the right-of-way had been obstructed by the erection of a fence. The Council wrote to Lord Tweeddale's factor, Mr Swinton, telling him to have both the manure heap and the fence removed.

Three months passed. The factor had now written to explain that Mr James Ferguson had erected a railing around a piece of waste ground, in order to make it into a garden; and that Mr Swinton had ordered Mr Ferguson to remove both the railing and the manure heap. About this time, Mr Swinton, the factor, retired. So the Parish Council took up the issue with the new factor, Mr McDonald. The paper trail seems to end there but, a century later, the public footpath survives.

A Threat of Invasion, 1804

A 200-year-old newspaper, found beneath floorboards during renovations in 2005 at the Plough Hotel, Yetholm, reports at length preparations by Napoleon to invade Britain. The newspaper consists of eight pages of the *Edinburgh Weekly Journal*, dated 29 February 1804. Though generally in poor condition, large areas remain readable.

In 1804 Britain was at war with France. This was the year before Trafalgar, and the newspaper reports efforts by Lord Nelson to meet up with the French fleet. George III was on the throne, and the newspaper reports an improvement in his health [the monarch was mentally deranged, and six years later the Prince of Wales would be appointed Regent. The King died in 1820.] A defiant editorial on the war declares: *"The Boaster [Napoleon], who is said to visit Boulogne every three weeks, must frequently have experienced how much his vaunted efforts are despised, and, knowing that his squadrons at Brest and the Texel are hermetically sealed up, he must, if his mad ambition can know an interval of sanity, feel the absurdity of attacking an entire nation, determined to die in the last ditch of European freedom."* In the section of the newspaper devoted to events at sea, the Journal states: *"It is very confidently reported that the Toulon squadron has given Lord Nelson the slip and put to sea; and that his Lordship was left in chase of it, and with a fair prospect of coming up with it."*

There was little new to communicate on the health of the King, the editorial added. His Majesty's health seemed in a state of progressive improvement, and encouraged the most sanguine expectations of its speedy and complete re-establishment. No communication had yet been made to Parliament on the subject, and it was hoped none would now be necessary.

Hospital Service, 1865

One day in the 1990s Mr Robin Butler, Kirk Yetholm, was carrying out repairs to a house when he discovered in a wall cavity a grubby document, which proved to be the report for 1864-65 of the Royal Infirmary of Edinburgh.

Edinburgh Royal Infirmary was remarkable at that time in that, almost a century before a National Health Service was thought of, this hospital with a national reputation for excellence was sustained by voluntary contributions from individuals, communities and organisations throughout Scotland, including the Borders.

The list of Managers includes Professor Sir James Young Simpson, Bart., pioneer in the use of chloroform in surgery. Another office-bearer is Dr Joseph Bell, of Edinburgh University, whose powers of observation inspired a young Arthur Conan Doyle to invent Sherlock Holmes.

Personal subscriptions in town and country came from all over Scotland, including the most northerly counties of Caithness, Orkney and Shetland.

The report expresses the Managers' obligations to the Local Treasurers in country parishes, who did so much to add to the revenue of the Infirmary. The high degree of organisation in the fund-raising is shown by the list of Local Treasurers in county parishes. This list shows well over 200 names –0 local ministers, schoolmasters, lawyers, bankers, postmasters – who acted for the Infirmary in this respect. There were annual collections in 17 counties, from Roxburgh to Shetland. In Yetholm, the Local Treasurer was James Henderson, registrar; in Morebattle, he was John Swanson, schoolmaster.

There were 124 Infirmary in-patients that year whose usual residence was in the Border counties (of whom 41 were from Roxburghshire, including two from Yetholm).

In addition to community fund-raising, the report records the names and addresses of literally hundreds of individuals throughout Scotland who made donations that year, the sums recorded being as small as five shillings. Income was also derived, of course, from organisations – insurance companies, railway companies, factory owners, newspaper proprietors, the police force, churches and chapels.

Individual donors in Yetholm included John B. Boyd., of Cherrytrees; the Rev. Adam Davidson; and Peter Govenlock.

There are a number of surprising items of expenditure. Articles of maintenance include: Beer, £199 17s 3d (compared with £140 7s 6d on Soap). Then there is Port Wine, 3 pipes (£160 10s); Sherry, 275 gallons (£151 5s); Champagne, 2 pints (4s); Whisky, (£42); Gin (£25 4s); Brandy, (£106 11s); Lemonade and ginger beer (£29 15s 6d); Porter (£63 16s 6d); and Ale, (£35 4s).

Whether this outlay on strong drink was incurred for the benefit of the patients or the office-bearers, or both, is not recorded.

A Rudimentary Welfare System

It comes as no surprise that the system under which the poor of Yetholm were cared for in the 19th and early 20th centuries was elementary by any modern standard. The welfare system at that time was a matter of co-operation between the Church and, latterly, Yetholm Parish Council, and was funded by an assessment made upon the heritors and other property owners or tenants.

The Rev. William Blackie, writing in 1797, reported[1] that the number of poor on the roll in that year was usually about 30, each of whom received between 2s 6d and 2s 8d per week. Apart from those on the roll, some needy families received occasional help. The funding, obtained chiefly from assessments, had amounted in 1795 to £52 19s sterling. There was also the money from church collections, but this amounted to only about £8 annually, and it was given to indigent persons not on the poor roll, the idea being to keep them off the roll for as long as possible.

Some forty years later, the Rev. John Baird reported[2] that the number of poor upon the roll in Yetholm was "very great". He calculated that during the previous seven years, the average number of such persons receiving parochial relief had been 65.

The average sum raised yearly by assessment (half paid by the heritors, and half by tenants) had been £252 8s 10d, he said. The average sum, therefore, which each pauper received per year was £3 17s 6d.

---

[1] *Statistical Account of Scotland*, 1791-1799.

[2] *New Statistical Account of Scotland*, 1845.

Apart from that, the kirk session might have a sum of £15 to £20 at its disposal, of which £12 to £15 came from collections at church. This was distributed by the kirk session at its discretion among the poor, whether they were on the roll or not. Mr Baird noted: "It is unfortunate that, with very few exceptions, there is little disposition among the poor to refrain from seeking parochial aid; neither do they seem to consider it in any sense as degrading."According to Mr Baird, Yetholm also had an immigration problem. One great cause of the high number of poor in the parish, he said, was the facility with which aged and single persons, who had probably spent their lives in England, could procure a room or lodging in Yetholm: they subsisted by their own labour for a number of years and then, when unable to work, got themselves enrolled on the permanent list of poor. The consequence was an excessive proportion of pauperism, he said.

Mr Baird had a novel if rather drastic solution: this was to reduce the number of houses in Yetholm. To diminish the number of houses, he suggested, would be to diminish the vice and pauperism of the parish.

In 1845 Parliament passed a Poor Law (Scotland) Act, and this was one of the pieces of legislations under which Yetholm Parish Council governed locally. In July 1897, for example, the Council's minutes show that there were a total of 25 names on the poor roll, of which 16 were resident in Yetholm Parish. The rate awarded to individuals ranged from 2 shillings to 10 shillings a week.The following year, the Parish Council had before it a report from Kelso, written by Mr Alex. Stewart, the Visiting Officer of the Local Government Board. His report stated in part: "A few years ago the Inspector has had as many as 180 applications for relief in the year; by a judicious offer of the Poorhouse these applications have now been reduced to between 60 and 70… The number of Paupers in this parish is high, one in 25.2…"

The above may be a reference to the Poorhouse in Kelso, in which paupers in Yetholm might be offered a place. For most of these paupers, the poorhouse was not an attractive option, whether because of the regime there, or the uprooting from familiar surroundings, or the shame.

Extracts from the Yetholm Parish Council minutes[3] are illuminating.

3 November 1905: "A request by Nellie Herbert for clothing for her twin children was granted, but the Inspector was instructed to give only such cloth as was required for the under clothing, with a view to its being made into clothing by the mother."

---

[3] *Scottish Borders Archive & Local History Centre*, Selkirk

26 April 1906: "In view of the lodging house at Kirk Yetholm being abolished, the Inspector was authorised to agree to A. Douglas' offer of accommodation for any casual at an annual rent of thirty shillings per annum. The Inspector was instructed to inform Douglas that no other vagrants were to be allowed to occupy the room except those sent by the Inspector."

Evidently Mr Douglas was holding out for more than thirty shillings per annum.

12 May 1906: "The Clerk was instructed to offer Andrew Douglas fifty shillings as rent of room if he would take in the Casual Cases (Vagrants) sent by the Inspector."

22 May 1906: "The Clerk reported that he had been unable to get the room in Douglas' house as a Sickhouse. He was instructed to ask the Rev. W. Carrick Miller [the parish minister] if he would rent the stable in his possession for the purpose."

An Artist of Horse Power

The Rev. John Baird's only son achieved national distinction as a painter. This was Nathaniel Hughes John Baird, who was born in the manse at Kirk Yetholm in 1854. His mother was the minister's second wife, Bessie Hughes. His father was himself celebrated as the Scottish gipsies' advocate, and Nathaniel recalled gipsies coming and going freely about the manse virtually all the time. Baird's talent as a painter of the farm horse has probably never been equalled. Paintings of thoroughbred racehorses by others are a commonplace, but Baird loved to depict men and horses at their labours on the farm – at the plough, or drawing the hay waggon.

He was a fine draughtsman and a master of colour, and his horses are powerful and realistic. He was fond of depicting these magnificent animals at day's end, singly or in groups, returning to the stable and the cottage. It is significant that Baird was recording the immemorial role of the farm horse at a time when it was soon to end for ever, to be replaced by the engine and the tractor. In his young days Nathaniel studied art at Coldstream, Edinburgh and Paris, and after his marriage he and his wife moved to Devon in the early 1870s. On the death of his wife in 1919, he and their two children moved to Rodmell, Sussex. Baird has been described as of medium build, wiry, and reserved in manner. He smoked a pipe, never wore glasses, hated social gatherings and was a man of few words. He was elected a member of the Royal Academy, and there are many of his paintings in public collections, particularly in Canada and the United States. Apart from his landscapes, he also found success as a painter of portraits of the famous, including the novelist, Agatha Christie. He died at Reading in 1936.

Worthies of the Past

Several village characters, well known in their time, were described many years later, in the 1930s, by a writer, "D.P.", who evidently had been brought up in Yetholm and could recall events of the 1880s.

Jimmie Leech, a weaver who believed that Britain should be a republic, would stand on Yetholm Green, denouncing the iniquities of monarchy, with passionate fluency, to a non-existing audience. "The late General Wauchope once noted Jimmie delivering an oration, and wondered much that the orator could proceed to such heights of eloquence, without the stimulus of hearers. To a generation that does not recall Jimmie, it should be explained that he did not lack an inner 'stimulus' on such occasions. If he was not 'in the spirit', the spirit was undoubtedly in him!"

There were six brothers in the Cairns family who owned Blunty's Mill, and each brother was a character in his own right. Tom Cairns, who was less sturdily built than the others, was known for his picturesqueness of speech and could be the best of company. In 1893, "D.P." visited Yetholm accompanied by a friend who, one warm Sunday morning, found the heat of St James' Free Church unusually trying.

"My friend's starched collar showed little consistency by the time the service was over. Tom Cairns came forward to him and exclaimed at the church door: 'Man, ye're a graun' 'sweeter'! The incident impressed Tom, and years afterwards he recalled it as we stood on Yetholm Bridge. 'I min' that day' he said reflectively. 'It was an unco het day, in fac' it was a maist redeeklus het day, an' he was comin' oot o' the kirk wi' the blobs o' sweet fair spewin' oot o' him!'"

On another occasion Tom, dispensing hospitality at home for his friend, 'D.P.', was pouring a cup of tea. "He filled my cup to overflowing. 'Hold, enough' I cried, as the tea fell in a cascade over the cup's side. 'Man' said Tom, with the teapot still elevated. 'I'm like Geordie Lees, the cooper. Geordie reckoned he likit a gude fu' cup and a gey slutter in the saucer!'"

"Tom was a sermon taster, often vivid and devastating in his criticisms. He and I suffered one morning under an elderly minister, a visitor to Yetholm, who seemed remarkably well pleased with his own utterances. "'Whit did ye think o' that auld dromedary?' said Tom to me afterwards. I remarked that the preacher did not seem to stand greatly in need of outside commendation. 'Na' said Tom with conviction 'ye could juist see by the way he rase on his taes an' went back on his heels, and his openin' an' shutting' his een, hoo graun' it was tae himsel.'"

The evangelical note in Free Church life awakened a quick response in Jim, one of the younger Cairns brothers. Jim was alert and sturdy and in his young days his hair curled close to his head. Hair and beard were a deep shade of auburn.

"We often foregathered at 'tent meetings' on Yetholm Green, and the last time I saw him he left an open-air gathering one Sunday afternoon on the Haugh to accompany me to Bowmont Crescent. He enjoyed appreciation of his work done faithfully and disinterestedly, and I recall the pride with which he used to display the watch and chain presented to him for his long and efficient service as precentor in the Free Kirk."

"Peter Cairns, known as Pete, was the one brother who was clean shaven. He had a special predilection for the razor, and waxed indignantly in my presence once when the inoffensive town of Coldstream was mentioned. "'It's a maist extraordinary thing' he said 'but there's no' a place where ye can get a shave in the hale toon o' Cau'stream!' To Peter the deficiency appeared to be a flagrant oversight on somebody's part."

The Rescue of Agnes Scott

The mill lade that once served Yetholm's corn mills and Blunty's Mill could be hazardous. In November 1902, the police constable at Kirk Yetholm, William Burnett, reported to his Chief Constable a number of complaints from the public.

The common complaint was that if you were walking from Kirk Yetholm to Town Yetholm on a dark night, you had to watch your step as you came down the hill on passing Yetholm Mill. P.C. Burnett explained that in that situation, a person was apt to miss the end of the bridge over the lade and walk over the edge of a dyke into the water. This involved a fall of no less than nine feet.

This is exactly what happened one night to unfortunate Agnes Scott, a laundry maid. She walked right over the dyke and plunged into the water.

Fortunately her cries were heard by the parish minister, the Rev. William Carrick Miller, who was in the manse nearby. He found her in the water in a bewildered condition, trying to get up the dyke. The minister assisted her out and escorted her home. Agnes escaped with bruises but, added P.C. Burnett, had she been rendered unconscious by the fall she would have been drowned, as there was always about nine inches of water running in the mill race.

There was no fence to prevent such accidents; and this is the point on which everyone then started to pass the buck. The police constable spoke first to the miller, Mr Thomas Whitelaw. Mr Whitelaw said he could say nothing until he saw Mr Swinton, the factor to the Marquess of Tweeddale.

About a week later Mr Swinton (who incidentally lived at Gifford in East Lothian) said it wasn't up to him to erect a fence; it was the duty of the Road Trustees to fence a road. The Chief Constable wrote to Mr Stormonth Darling, the County Clerk, at Kelso. Mr Stormonth Darling passed the papers to Mr Tait, the District Clerk, who got in touch with Mr McBain, the Surveyor of Roads and Bridges.

Mr McBain visited the site of the accident, drew a helpful sketch of the lade, the bridge and the road – and then added defensively: "The woman wandered off the road before getting into the lade…" It was, he seems to be saying, nothing to do with him; any expenditure on a fence wasn't coming out of *his* budget.

Who eventually acted to ensure the public safety is not revealed in the correspondence files of the Borders Archive, Selkirk, where the story is told. But the once hazardous road today has a footpath for pedestrians, is well lit, and the lade is dry.

Policing the Village

Yetholm has not had a police station since 1980. The station had moved around the village during the previous 120 years: the Ordnance Survey map of 1863, for example, identifies Cheviot Villa, in the Crescent, Town Yetholm as the County Police Station. By 1898, however, the station had been moved along the Crescent to Craiglea, where the Post Office is now.

Earlier in the 19th century there was a police station in Kirk Yetholm, and indeed the police authorities rented the cottage from Mr Peter Govanlock, who owned much else in Kirk Yetholm besides.

Being a country policeman between the two World Wars must have been very different from policing nowadays. Old men now recall that when they were boys, the police constable had a set routine as he pedalled round the neighbourhood on his bicycle: as a result, the boys knew exactly where he was at any time, and made sure they were somewhere else.

A new police station was built at the top of Dow Brae in 1969. At that time, Yetholm and Morebattle had one police officer stationed in each village; Morebattle police station was subsequently closed, and both officers moved into the new building at Yetholm,

When Yetholm police station closed in 1980, the last two officers stationed there were P.C. Howlett and P.C. Goodall, who were transferred to Kelso. The building was sold, along with the police houses, in 1988.

Chapter 10

Commercial Life

The Shops

Almost from its inception in 1994, Yetholm History Society began to compile a list of the many shops that had flourished in the village. There were at least 20 of these family retail businesses, at one time or another, and the objective of the Society's project was to record their history, averting a danger that as time passed the shops and their owners would be forgotten altogether. Other businesses in the village were similarly catalogued.

Apart from valuation rolls, and the occasional newspaper advertisement, documentary evidence is sparse, and so we have been dependent on personal recollection by older residents. Allowance must be made for the fallibility of memory, particularly where dates are concerned. The essay is as accurate as we can make it. Our study is ongoing, and the record will be refined as new evidence comes to hand.

There Were So Many

Because many of the shops operated within what were originally designed as cottages, most of them were small and quite different from the conventional, purpose-built shops we know today.

That there were so many viable shops in Town Yetholm, and indeed in Kirk Yetholm too, reflects the fact that even midway through the 20th century the village was a more close-knit community, more self-sufficient. Without leaving the village you could have a suit made by a tailor, buy a new pair of shoes, have your watch repaired, and purchase many kinds of linen drapery, either for the household or for personal use. There were several grocers, butchers, at least two baker shops, a chemist, sweet shops, and newsagents, and on the way home you could buy a fish supper.

Yetholm shops delivered ordered goods to the outlying farms, and businesses based elsewhere paid weekly visits to Yetholm to sell from the back of a van.

Long before the advent of the Planning Acts, opening a shop seems to have been a simple matter: you converted one of the rooms in your house, then advertised the fact by nailing a wooden sign above the front door. Your front window could be used to display the goods.

The day of the horse on the farm might be passing, but there was still enough work for the Gladstones' smithy, and for John Allan's saddlery, as well as the motor garages of Gibson, and Stenhouse, serving an increasing number of vehicles.

There was no permanent bank branch, but at least two of the Scottish banks paid a weekly visit, renting someone's front room to enable their customers to transact business.

Why did almost all of the shops disappear? One factor more influential than any other was the increase in private car ownership. Throughout the country, families became more mobile, and as they acquired their own wheels, they shopped much more widely. Subsequently, the advent of supermarkets in the nearby towns spelled doom for the viability of all but a handful of village shops.

Some Family Businesses

People setting up shop in Town Yetholm in the old days favoured the east side of the main street, between the top of Dow Brae and the premises of Lees the butcher. On that frontage we have identified a succession of 16 shopkeepers – five grocers, four bakers, one butcher and six other shops.

The individual shops came and went, as the family circumstances of the owners waxed and waned. Those shops that were there in the 19th century were viable in the main because the village was secluded to a degree that is hard to imagine now in our age of mass communication.

The busiest and best remembered of the Yetholm shops seems to have been the prominent licensed grocer which operated successfully for many years, under a succession of owners, before the shop closed and became the Paramount Guest House about 1969. It operated as a guest house until 2005.

An early owner of this grocery store was Henry Thomas Davidson, who was a grocer in the village from at least 1869 until about 1905. Then it was run by William F. Armstrong from then until about 1934, and in its heyday by William Hardie and his wife, Robina.

Before the Second World War Hardie's grocery had been on the other side of the main street, immediately south of where Gibson's Garage is today. He moved to the premises on the east side of the street about 1934. The Hardies disposed of their business when Mr Hardie retired in 1949. The Sibbald family was the last to have the shop, and when Mr Sibbald retired in 1968 the shop closed.

The winter of 1947 was hard, with deep snow across the country. Normal deliveries by Hardie's the grocer to outlying farms were impossible. So Madge the Clydesdale pulled a field sled from the Bowmont Valley to collect supplies. (Photo by the late Bessie Martin, who worked in the shop).

There is a well known photograph of Hardie's, taken by the late Bessie Martin during the hard winter of 1947. In normal times Hardie's regularly sent a motor van to deliver round the farms in the Bowmont Valley and its vicinity, but during the severe winter, deep snow blocked roads for 11 weeks.

The horse and sled in the photograph are from Sourhope, and this was the only way in which essential supplies could be collected.

Bessie Martin, who had come to Yetholm with her parents in May 1943, was employed at Hardie's from then until 1949. Bessie's fellow assistants behind the counter included Isobel Dickson [Paterson] who lived at Hayhope; Edith Spence, who was originally from Newcastle; and Betty Christie, daughter of John Christie the joiner, whose workshop was at Rosebank at the north end of the village.

When winter ended, Hardie's resumed delivering by van to the surrounding villages and farms, and part of Bessie's duties was to help deliver orders. On Thursdays and Fridays the van delivered to the Bowmont Valley, while Saturdays was delivery day to Kirk Yetholm. The more isolated customers up the Bowmont Valley settled their bills with Hardie's every six months.

When the Hardies retired in 1949 the business was acquired by William Sibbald and his wife, Nora. The breadth of the service offered by Mr Sibbald is illustrated by his commercial advertisement in 1959: "Grocers, provisions, teas and coffee, wine and spirits, fruit and vegetables, drapery and furnishings, ironmongery, glass and china."

Mr Sibbald was elected to Roxburgh County Council in 1964, and after he retired from the business in 1968, the premises reverted to a private dwelling. Mr Sibbald moved his home to North Berwick, East Lothian, where he died in July 1999, aged 93.

One of the most distinctive dwellings on the east side of the main street – a picturesque thatched cottage north of the Plough Hotel – is still well remembered as a newspaper and sweet shop run by several elderly ladies, including the Wait sisters. However, the first mention of commercial activity on this property is much earlier, when there was a bakehouse at the rear.

Research of the property records[1] indicates that a John Scott, baker, was using part of the building as a bakehouse not later than 1863. In 1875, Mr Scott was followed by another baker, John Kerr. Mr Kerr died in 1909, and it is not clear if the bakery continued after that date.

In 1920 the lease was bought by a timber merchant, Charles Thomas Dowey. There is still no mention of the front of the house being sub-divided to create shop premises. In 1921 the Wait family enter the picture, the lease being sold to Miss Helen Wait. She used part of the ground floor as a newsagent and confectionery shop. Miss Wait is described as a dressmaker in some valuation rolls.

Miss Wait died about 1956, leaving the property to two nieces, Miss Agnes and Miss Betty Bonnington. Miss Wait's nephew, James Abernethy, a market gardener, then became tenant and subsequently owner; the part of the property used as a shop was kept by his sister, Agnes ("Nessie") Abernethy, who also lived in the house. The shop was in the room to the left hand side of the front door, and at that time still had an earth floor.

James Abernethy died in 1974, and in 1980 the thatched cottage passed out of the family's ownership, Nessie having become a resident of Romany House, the former hotel which became for a number of years a care home run by the local authority. About the same time (i.e. 1980) all visible traces of the shop were removed and the house returned to its earlier sole use as a dwelling.

---

[1] By Mr and Mrs Dancey.

Harden Cottage, near the top of Dow Brae, was occupied in the 1930s and 1940s by Richard Stenhouse, baker.

The Border Boot Store was run by John Wakeford for about 30 years. An enterprising man, Mr Wakeford was originally a roadman and had watched John Watson's grandfather cobbling in Huntsman's Cottage. Thus versed in the skills of the trade, he began on his own, at first in one of the thatched cottages (now gone) that were on a corner by Dow Brae. Then he moved his business a few doors along the street. John Wakeford died in April 1961, in his 80th year, and the Border Boot Store closed in the early 1960s.

Tice the baker was another well-known shop on the east side of the street. The premises were bought by Mr George Tice in the 1890s from Mr John Kerr, for whom he had worked initially. George Tice had two sons, Richard (Ritchie) and Garnet. George Tice died in February 1940, aged 80. The family bakery business, which was particularly famed for the tastiness of its pies, continued at this location until 1957, when it was moved to the Crescent, immediately south of Adams' store. The bakery business continued there until 1969. Ritchie Tice died in April of the following year. His brother Garnet, who lived on until November 1987, took a prominent part in village events, notably the gipsy coronation re-enactment in 1959.

Greystone House was the shop of Robert Chalmers, jeweller and watch maker. He had a shop there from 1894, and died at Selkirk in August 1926 in his 66th year. He was a widower, his wife Mary White Young having died at Yetholm in April 1913.

Hudson House (adjacent to Ivy Cottage). Jas Turnbull was a boot and shoe maker, and his son, James Dixon Turnbull, had a small grocer's shop here in the mid 1930s. His daughter, Mrs Elma Goodfellow, lives in Ivy Cottage.

The shop occupied today by George Lees' butcher business has had at least two previous tenants. At the start of the 1930s it was occupied by a shoemaker, Danny Robertson, and was also used by George Cairns, a village tailor and clothier, who earlier had begun business life at Montgomerie Place. Mr Cairns was to move once more, this time to premises immediately north of the Wauchope Hall. The Robertson family later moved their business to the Horsemarket, Kelso.

The butcher business was founded by George Lees' father (also George) in Morebattle in 1912. He expanded to Yetholm about 1922, his first shop in this village being a wooden building just around the corner from the shop familiar today. It was about 1941 before the present-day shop was opened.

On the west side of the main street, across the road from the butchers', Huntsman Cottage was once the shoe shop of John Watson senior. Dalveen was a butcher's run by Tommy Simpson: the killing-house was round the corner, off the side street. Mr Simpson was retired by 1930.

In the side street there was a Good Templars' Hall, a temperance society, with an outside stair leading to a flat. This was where the Boy Scout troop in Yetholm started. The Scouts moved later to an upstairs room in the former brewery, and then to the Scout Hall, now re-named the Youth Hall.

Rose Cottage, further along the main street, was run as a tearoom by the Misses Murphy about 1959.

On the west side of the main street, there were a number of shops that have now gone.

The private house situated immediately to the south of Gibson's Garage has been in the past a shop and also the village post office.

Yetholm post office has operated in at least three different places in the past 150 years, of which this seems to have been the first: it is identified as the village post office on maps of 1853 and 1898. In the 1851 national census, the postmaster was James Laidlaw, aged 25. He was living in this household with his parents and other members of the family: his shopkeeper father, Robert, was a baker, grocer and spirit merchant. Robert Laidlaw died in July 1863, aged 65.

By 1871 James had charge of the business, describing himself as a general merchant. He was now married, and he and his wife Annie had two daughters and one son. Sadly, Annie died in February 1878, at the early age of 33. By 1891 James, now 65 years of age, was still a general merchant. Obviously regarded as a person of standing in the community, he had served for some years as a member of the School Board. He died in September 1897, aged 70. His last surviving daughter, Catherine Jane, died in March 1947, aged 72.

In the 20th century the shop and post office in this property were run by a succession of families, including a Turner and T.J. Marshall. The premises were also occupied by Mr Willie Hardie the grocer for a time, before

This is the shop, immediately south of the garage, run by Francis Christie's family from about 1936 until the early seventies.

he moved his business to larger premises across the street in succession to W.F. Armstrong.

John W. Christie and his family took over the premises about 1936, and continued it for 36 years until the introduction of decimalisation of the coinage. They were followed by a Mr Bell and a Mr Johnston. At that period, lighting and heating in Yetholm depended heavily on paraffin: Christie's van might deliver as much as 50 gallons of paraffin each week.

During the Second World War the importing of bananas was banned by the Government as inefficient use of shipping space. Consequently, at the end of hostilities, the re-appearance of bananas caused something of a sensation, particularly among young children who had never seen one. Christie's ordered a consignment from a wholesaler in Glasgow and gave away the bananas to their customers, the number given varying according to the total value of goods purchased.

Subsequently the shop was operated for a number of years by members of the Stewart family, who carried on with a milk delivery service which covered a large area of the countryside. It included two villages, numerous hill farms and continued on up the valley to Hownam. After eight years the shop closed in 1986, when it reverted to a private dwelling. [2]

---

[2] Research by Mrs Ivy Elder

Adams' shop as it appeared before the large display windows were installed. The newspaper billboards suggest the photo was taken after the Second World War.

Immediately north of the Wauchope Hall were premises that served a number of traders. The earliest that we know of was George Bell, grocer and wine merchant, who was followed by other grocers, John Somerville and his wife Janet, who were there between the two world wars. Scott's of Kelso was there for a brief period, before George Cairns, the tailor and draper, moved here about 1940 from the other end of the village. In the 1980s the premises were opened again as a grocery by John and Mary Watson. More recently the premises were those of Country Cuts, hairdresser.

The handsome Victorian villa, "Montana" is believed to have been built by an Edinburgh solicitor. Thereafter it had a number of owners or occupiers. It was for a time the shop of a butcher who reportedly sold only mutton. Then it was at one time Tommy Hawkins' barber shop. After he gave up business, the house was occupied by an Italian family. They made fried chips in an outbuilding at the rear and sold them over a counter in a front room. The doorway of this shop can still be traced in the wall. The property was also at one time a tea garden run by Mr JohnWagstaffe, who had been a butler to a millionaire in America, and whose anecdotes about life in the U.S. were enjoyed by young and old. The local library was also here for a while after being in a thatched house where the entrance to Gibson's Garage is now.

Gibson's Garage, constructed after the Second World War, replaced a two-storey thatched building, which was shared by three families. The Gibson family took over the small garage (and taxi business) from Johnny Stenhouse when he retired: the garage at that time was still situated across the road and down the slope, towards the school.

Twizel House, between Adams' shop and the vennel, marks the point at which the main street becomes The Crescent. Twizel House was a shop for a time, about the beginning of the 20th century. This came to light on examination of a historic photograph, taken on the day the Wauchope Memorial was unveiled on the Green. In the background of the photograph can be seen spectators standing in the doorway of Twizel House. Above the front door is a sign, "Grahamslaw, grocer".

The Village Shop[3] and the Lees' butcher shop are the survivors of a retail consolidation trend that affected virtually all the shops that once flourished in Town Yetholm. The Adams' business connection with the village began as a tailor's shop. John V. Adams, who had moved to Yetholm from the east of Scotland early in the 20th century, was a tailor and practised his trade in the village from about 1910. The family's career in retail began with the selling of soft drinks, sweets and newspapers from a wooden building around the corner from Lees' butcher shop.

In the early years of the shop in the Crescent there were no big display windows as there are today: historical photos show that at that time Adams' shop retained a conventional house frontage, which incorporated domestic windows. To the right was the house door, leading to the dwelling house. When the display windows were installed at some point before 1971, these replaced the house door as well as the original windows. For a year or two the shop had a tearoom upstairs, which was reached by an internal spiral stair.

Greenbank, adjacent to Adams' shop, was at one time the village Post Office (which has had at least three different homes). The post office was in a room to the left of the door; you could collect your mail from a room to the right. The village telephone switchboard was here, and in those days, a phone number in Yetholm might have only one or two digits. About 1930 the postmistress was Mrs Annette Walker.

The house in the Crescent now known as Saddler's Cottage had a connection with the trade of saddlery which can be traced back to 1894. In that year the proprietor is recorded as Robert Allan, saddler, and he continued to have a shop there until 1925. He was succeeded by John Allan, who was also the postman in the village. John could repair clocks, and he seemed to be able to turn his hand to anything. He possessed a model railway, which he probably made himself. By 1934 the proprietors of the cottage were Helen and Cecilia Allan.

---

[3] In 2006 the Adams family sold the business to Mr and Mrs Roy and Barbara Maltby, who re-named the shop.

Food prices: Shillings and Pennies

The many shops that flourished in Yetholm in the first half of the 20th century played an essential role in the annual Shepherds' Show. Yetholm History Society has an interesting collection of invoices sent out to the Show organisers and participants in the years 1923, 1924 and 1925.

The invoices show clearly the extent to which money values have altered in the past eighty years! Even if we assume that the businessmen may have been discounting their normal charges because the Shepherds' Show was a traditional annual event, the low level of their invoices is remarkable.

For example, after the 1923 Show Andrew Bulman, of Kelso, submitted the following to the organisers: "To hire of tent marquee at Show, including time of joiners fitting up same: £2." October 1923: Alex. Young, carrier: "To removing tents and tables to and from Haugh: 12 shillings"; and a bag of coal, 2s 6d.

For an advertisement about the teas available at that Show, the *Kelso Chronicle* charged 5s.

Many of the invoices in the collection refer to the YMCA Club, whose home was in the building that is now the Youth Hall. Because of its nationally familiar logo, the club was also known as the Red Triangle Club. Members of the Daw family were closely associated with the Red Triangle, which always had a tent at the Shepherds' Show. It was at the 1923 event that the YMCA tent took delivery of a consignment of food from Richard Stenhouse the baker, which included 12 dozen of Richie's famous pies (at 3s per dozen).

In October 1924 George Lees the butcher supplied the Red Triangle Club with 17 lbs of salt beef and an 11 lb roast, for which the club was charged a grand total of £1 17s 8d.

In the same year George Tice the baker charged 3d per pie, and the YMCA club ordered 12 dozen of them.

It was at the 1924 event that the refreshment tent ordered 1 stone of sugar (i.e. 14 lbs) from Mr W.F. Armstrong, the licensed grocer (total cost, 5s 10d). 1 lb of tea was an additional 2s 6d.

In 1925 it was the turn of Robert Nichol & Son to erect and remove the Red Triangle Club tent (cost, £1 10s).

October 1925: George Lees the butcher: 26 3/8 lbs salt brisket @ 1s 4d per lb: £1 15s 2d. Plus a 12 lb. roast and 6 steaks, £1 6s.

Still more pies (obviously universally popular) were sold to the YMCA tent for the 1925 Show by baker Richie Stenhouse: 6 dozen for 18s. Plus currant loaves, iced slab cake, seed cake, sultana cake, ginger cake, jam rolls, more cake, as well as white bread and brown bread. Total bill: £4 14s 6d.

In 1925 the YMCA tent obtained their stone of sugar from John Somerville the grocer (4s 8d). But the Red Triangle Club needed a further stone of sugar that month, this time from T.J. Marshall the family grocer (4s 8d).

Before we start pining for the days of such low prices, however, the 1920s were hard days, with the average wage no more than a few pounds per week.

Banking Days

There were weekly visits by at least two of the Scottish banks, each of which rented a room in order to conduct business with their customers.

The British Linen Bank used premises near the north end of the Crescent – Allan the saddler, or perhaps Greenbank, once a week from about 1960 to about 1980.

Another bank used a room in the Temperance Hotel (the building now occupied by Cheviot House and Eildon House, adjacent to the Plough.)

It is said that on occasion the proprietor of the Temperance Hotel, Mr David Riddell, who was a retired gamekeeper, would sit outside the door of the hotel, with a shotgun across his knees!

The banks' weekly visits ceased, it is believed, not for lack of business but because of increased concern about security between Yetholm and Kelso.

One person recalled that the Royal Bank of Scotland had used a room in the Waits' thatched cottage.

Haunts of Rare Souls

At the time of writing there are two inns in Yetholm and no ale houses. It was not always so; the census return of 1851 recorded 7 innkeepers and in 1834, in the New Statistical Account of Scotland, the Rev. John Baird had noted three or four inns in Town Yetholm and three inns in Kirk Yetholm. Some of these furnish accommodation for travellers. Besides these there are also seven ale houses where ale and spirits are sold. The innkeepers in Town Yetholm were John Kerr, Alexander Dodds, Thomas Jackson, and in Kirk Yetholm were found James Wilson, Robert Dickson, Janet Richardson, and Christine Govanlock, the mother of Peter, who was to acquire much property in Yetholm.

In the Statistical Account 1791-1799, the earlier recorder, the Rev William Blackie, failed to mention any inns or ale houses or the illicit commerce of smuggling whisky which Baird had said formerly gave employment and subsistence to one-fifth or one-sixth of the inhabitants of the two villages.

There is little doubt that in those times the clergy did not favour inns and particularly ale houses. In Roxburghshire they recorded:

"they are of an injurious influence on the lower orders", (Lilliesleaf).

"the effects on the morals of the people are most pernicious", (Melrose).

"they present far too great a facility to dissipation", (St Boswells).

"their existence is productive of decided evil", (Crailing).

And so on.

Baird himself made no moral judgements, apart from the illicit smuggling of whisky which he thought "must have a demoralising influence".

Not all the comments on drinking habits were adverse, however. In Denholm was found a more favourable view ; the inns "are regarded as an advantage, and, in general, it is not understood that any of these houses have had any demoralising effect". Always a major part of social life throughout the land, the inns, taverns and ale houses of the past have become the hotels and pubs of today and still bring mixed favour. Most provide pleasurable refreshment in convivial company.

The Yorkshireman J. B. Priestley wrote memorably of one inn as a "haunt of rare souls".

The Rev. Dr. John Gray, who lived in Kirk Yetholm as a boy in the 1920s in the house formerly The Cross Keys, recalled "five public houses in a village of some forty dwellings was a living memory in our day".

The word inn is derived from the Saxon meaning room. An inn provided rooms for travellers as well as providing food and ale.

Inns might be privately owned by the innkeeper, who was therefore the proprietor, or the property of some other person or a brewery where the innkeeper was the tenant. At times the inns of Yetholm were variously owned in such manner, whereas an ale house was usually the business venture of the resident; only ale and spirits were sold, food was not normally available and there were no rooms to let.

Brewing is a simple process, and by the 15th century domestic brewing, particularly in farming communities, became so widespread that a licence duty of four Scots pence a year was imposed on all persons engaged in brewing. Unlike today, brewing was usually woman's work, to which farming women took quite a liking. An ale house provided a lucrative income, the lady of the house served customers on the premises and sold drink to take out.

With the granting of licences to the toll houses (there were three in Yetholm), the houses providing refreshment were plentiful.

The days of the ale house are long gone and there are none in Yetholm today, and none are recalled in the memories of the village folk now.

Domestic brewing declined with the growth of the public breweries.

Yet in 1791 there was a maltster and three coopers in Yetholm as noted by Blackie, and Rutherfurd's Register in 1866 noted a maltster and a cooper, one George Lees, the great grandfather of the recently retired butcher of the same name in Town Yetholm.

In 1814, a breakaway group of the Kirk, the United Presbyterian Church, met in a building in Town Yetholm owned by a local brewer, Robert Elliott. This may have been the building at 3 Montgomerie Place known to all now as the "Old Brewery", yet there is no real evidence today that brewing was carried out there. The register of sasines describes it only as a warehouse or store. Although first recorded in a feu contract between Col. Andrew Gilbert Wauchope and Peter Govanlock on 26 June 1890, its only mention as "The Old Brewery" is in a Deed of Restriction on 28 February 1963.

The records show it was owned at various times by grocers who may have used it as a store for ales and spirits.

A map of Town Yetholm in 1859 marks the Plough Inn, the Swan Inn, which later became a house, and the Nag`s Head, which was a temperance hotel, and innkeeper John Scott, a baker.

Today the Swan Inn is recalled as the White Swan and was a popular "haunt of the rare souls" of Town Yetholm until its closure about 1982. The public bar was quite narrow by modern standards: it is said it was possible to sit on the bench against one wall and place your glass on the counter.

In 1866 the innkeeper was Thomas Inglis, and in 1869 the innkeeper was David Harkness and the proprietor was John Kerr (saddler). In 1884 the innkeeper was James Turnbull and the proprietor was Miss Helen Davidson. In 1900 the tenant was Mrs Jane Turnbull, proprietor Mrs Agnes Black, and by 1910 the innkeeper was Andrew Robson. Mr and Mrs Robson continued there throughout the 1920s and into the 1930s.

Between 1920 and 1950 the White Swan was owned, first by the Coldstream Brewery Co., and then by C. Vaux and Sons of Sunderland. In 1940 the tenant was John J. Johnston. In 1960 the tenant was Edward Ted Watson.

Like the Plough across the street, the White Swan was always part of the annual Fastern E'en Games. In February 1928, the *Kelso Chronicle* reported:
"After The Games the committee and officials sat down to a sumptuous tea in the White Swan Hotel, Mr and Mrs Robson doing everything they could to attend to the wants of the company".

The Plough Hotel, Town Yetholm, about 1890. The photograph has been carefully composed in order to promote the hotel's facilities. The innkeeper at that time, Mr George Brown, had been the tenant for at least six years. In the doorway stands the proprietrix or manageress (perhaps Mrs Brown). In the foreground the young lady, evidently wearing her best dress for the occasion, is either a daughter, or a member of staff, or both. On the right, in the horse-drawn brake, sits a young man, ready to drive to Mindrum Station, or if need be, to Kelso Station, to meet a train and collect guests who had reserved rooms at the Plough. The rather roughly dressed man on the left may be an employed handyman: had he been Mr George Brown, he surely would have worn a better suit for the photograph, and been allocated a position nearer the centre of things. (Photograph by permission of Hawick Museum).

The frontage of the Plough Inn was much shorter than it is today, with a gateway to the yard at the rear. In 1866 the innkeeper was James McCallum and the proprietor was Andrew Wauchope. In 1890 the innkeeper was George Brown, who had been the tenant since at least 1884. By 1900 it was owned by a firm of brewers in Berwick on Tweed, Johnson and Darlings Ltd, with Thomas Barnett the tenant.

In 1904 the innkeeper was R C Russell and by 1910 the innkeeper was William M. Badenoch. Between the two World Wars, Mrs Mary Martha Turnbull, a widow, was the innkeeper for at least a decade and perhaps longer. She was one of the principal financial supporters of the annual Bowmontside Games at Fastern E'en, with its traditional hand ba' match on the Haugh. By 1930 the proprietor was the Berwick Breweries Ltd. In 1940, one year into the Second World War, the innkeeper was John A Witty. By 1950, he had been succeeded by James Bowie. Later proprietors or tenants were D. Owens, George Beveridge (from March 1959), Mrs Dunn,

John Rowe, Albert Scott, Ian Angus (arrived 1984), Willie Cardwell (from August 1996), John Darling, and Maxine Wilson.

George Beveridge had become famous for breaking-in horses in his earlier days and originally handled the Grand National winner, Merryman II.

Diane and Andrew Hay became the innkeepers in June 2004.

In Kirk Yetholm, it has been noted that there was an inn called the Queen owned by the then King of the Gipsies, William Faa II (reigned 1784-1847), who was also famed for smuggling whisky over the border into England, and featured in the old rhyme:

"There's canny Wull Faa o' Kirk Yetholm,
He lives i' the sign o' the Queen
He got a great slash i' the hand
When coming frae Boulmer wi gin".

This inn is not marked on the map of Kirk Yetholm in 1859, yet is shown on a picture of similar time and was located near the Old Gypsy Palace on the north side of the High Street. The 1859 map marks the Gray Horse (later to become the Border Hotel), the Plough Inn of which only a few stones remain on the village green and not to be confused with the Plough Inn in Town Yetholm; the Cross Keys which later became a house; and the Shepherds Arms, which was a temperance hotel of which, in 1861, the innkeeper was Patrick Milligan, who was also a grocer.

In Kirk Yetholm, in 1861 the innkeeper of the Plough Inn was Janet Richardson, in 1869 the proprietor was William Mitchell jun., and the innkeeper was William Mitchell sen.

In 1869 the owner of the Cross Keys was Peter Govanlock and his tenant was George Collins.

By 1884 Peter Govanlock had become the owner of the Plough and the innkeeper was his sister, Miss H Govanlock, who had been listed in 1861 as the innkeeper of the Gray Horse, later to be known as The Border Inn.

By 1890 Peter had become the proprietor of the Gray Horse with "Ellen" continuing as the innkeeper. The Inn was acquired in 1893 by David Keddie, a brewer from Jedburgh, who installed Thomas Renalson as the landlord. For about the next 20 years the inn stayed in the ownership of David Keddie and his descendants and became known as the Border Inn or Hotel.

Sometime between 1893 and 1898, major alterations were carried out, an upstairs section was added with two gables and a tiled roof. Part of the original thatched inn was retained, which exists today.

Thomas Renalson was the innkeeper on 30 May 1898 on the famous occasion of the coronation of King Charles Faa Blythe, King of the Yetholm Gypsies. Thomas Renalson was an interesting character. Born in Jedburgh in 1853, he was an athlete of some note, awarded "The Lothian Cup" at the Jedburgh Games in 1880.

The *Jedburgh Gazette* of 16 July 1880 reported "Lothian Cup, confined to Border Counties Flat Race of 800 yards. First prize a handsome silver cup. T. Rennilson, Jedburgh, 32 yards, 13 ran, Rennilson came to the front in good form and reached the goal amid cheering". His brother John was a good runner too and came first in the 200 yards handicap for Jedburgh Youths under 18 at the Jedburgh Games in the following year, 1881 Thomas went to Australia with his parents, brothers and sister in 1882, sailing to Sydney on SS Samuel Plimsoll. By 1891 the family had returned to Jedburgh, though there is a relative, Stuart Renalson, in New Zealand today. From 1893 to 1890 Thomas was the landlord of the Border Hotel, where he died on 9 January 1900.

In 1900 Charles Horatio Lewis became the tenant and innkeeper.

In 1904 the innkeeper was Thomas Hosie and by 1910 the tenant was James Adams.

In 1920 the property was owned by Andrew Dunn, spirit merchant, Sunderland; his tenant was James Halliday.

By 1930 the proprietor and hotelkeeper was David Gustard Reah.

Between 1940 and 1950 the proprietor and hotelkeeper was Archibald T. Donaldson, succeeded by Gordon Townsend, a former pilot in Coastal Command during the Second World War, and then by Bill Ritchie.

In the years 1987 to 1995 the owners and innkeepers were Devon Russell and his wife Eileen. Devon Russell first saw the hotel when he arrived in Yetholm in 1942 as an eight-year-old evacuee from Tyneside. He fell in love with Yetholm and developed friendships which have lasted a lifetime. During the war he lived with Mrs. Underwood and her family. Her son, John, still lives in the village and his friendship with "Dev" endures.

The Border Hotel, about 1890. Mr Thomas Renalson became the innkeeper about this time, and was in that post on the famous occasion of the gipsy coronation in 1898. Earlier in the century the Border had been named the Gray Horse.

"Dev" spent half his life as a marine engineer on deep-sea vessels and Thames tugs, and then went ashore to run a docklands pub called the Flying Scud at Canning Town in London's East End. In 1995, Eileen and "Dev" retired again and returned south, though return each year to remind us.

The Border Hotel is famous as the hostelry which marks the end of the Pennine Way, the long distance walk which starts in Edale in Derbyshire and ends in Kirk Yetholm.

For many years anyone who could prove they had started the walk in Edale was entitled to a free pint of beer if they produced a copy of Wainwright's "Pennine Way Guide". This courtesy was introduced by Alfred Wainwright himself.

In "Dev's" words : "When Wainwright was alive we kept a fund behind the bar. It was a pretty free and easy arrangement and I wrote to him whenever the cash was running low". By the time Wainwright died aged 84 in 1991, he had paid for £ 12,000 of free beer. For a while the courtesy was taken over by Wainwright's publisher, Michael Joseph, and from time to time the tradition is revived by the landlord of the day.

In 1995 the hotel was acquired by Maxine Day during whose tenure further alterations were carried out with the addition of a conservatory and an extension containing four bedrooms and a dining/function room.

Margaret and Philip Blackburn became the innkeepers in May 2004.

At the time of writing, village folk recall other establishments which served as inns or ale houses. These were Romany House in Town Yetholm and The Halterburn Hotel or "Ponderosa".

Romany House became a home for the elderly, then returned to being a private house and guest house.

Originally a large farmhouse, the Halterburn Hotel became fully licensed in March 1965 and its "new Log Cabin Lounge Bar" was opened on 19 March. The renovation was carried out by a couple from Yorkshire, Douglas Mossman and his wife Elaine. With five double and one single bedroom, and "a trout stream twenty yards from the entrance", they hoped to attract the angling and shooting communities.

In the event it became a popular haunt of the rare souls from Yetholm.

Known to all as "The Ponderosa" on account of its resemblance to the ranch-house of that name in the TV series "Bonanza", this "rendezvous at the cabin in the hills" became the favourite place of the weekend crowd from Yetholm during the 1960s.

Fairly remote, yet easily accessible by motor-car on a narrow hill road, the end of its days as a night-out venue was hastened by the introduction of the breathalyser law on 9 October 1967, and it closed in 1968.

Since that time the house has been occupied by American evangelists Mr and Mrs Spencer Shellmyer, followed by another American, Mr Bradshaw, who provided missionary training. In more recent years it became a rehabilitation hostel or Penial Revival Centre run by Mr Bryan Wilson. This closed in early 2004.

Smuggling Days

In Scotland smuggling mainly involved whisky. The different tax regimes on spirits in England and Scotland encouraged the smuggling of whisky across the Border into England.

Kirk Yetholm was well situated for such trade which flourished with the smuggling of illegally distilled whisky and contraband salt brought over from Ireland which were stored in Yetholm and later transported by horseback on the green lanes through the Cheviot hills.

Smuggling also took place the reverse way, with illegally imported wines and brandy landed on the Northumberland coast.

In the 18th and 19th centuries smuggling became a major commercial activity for Yetholm folk. It was estimated that at least twenty percent or more of the population were involved in such trade.

Writing in the New Statistical Account of Scotland, 1845, the Rev. John Baird took a dim view of the trade of smuggling in Yetholm. He observed :
"The illegal practice of smuggling, till lately so prevalent in this neighbourhood, and so openly practised, must no doubt have had a very demoralising influence upon a considerable portion of the population; otherwise I am disposed to regard them as a quiet and well disposed people."

And further :
"There are no branches of commerce or manufacture carried on in this parish, with the exception, perhaps, of the illicit commerce of smuggling

whisky across the border, which, I have said, formerly gave employment and subsistence to one-fifth or one-sixth of the inhabitants of the two villages. Of this commodity, I am informed that from £10,000 to £20,000 worth annually have been sold from Yetholm into England in this manner; but now the quantity disposed of illegally for the English market is scarcely worth calculating. Within the last three or four years, effectual means have been taken by a stricter police, and by heavy fines imposed on delinquents, to put an end to this demoralizing and illicit traffic, which have succeeded in a great measure for the present."

Romany House

Romany House, a handsome Italianate villa in Morebattle Road, on the southern edge of Town Yetholm, was built about 1900 for Dr Alexander Rodger as a wedding present from his father. Dr Rodger was not only a medical practitioner but also held a degree in surgery.

He died on 27 November 1933, aged 62, and his widow, Dora Eugenie, died almost exactly ten years later. Both are interred in the churchyard at Kirk Yetholm.

In the following year the property was sold to Mr and Mrs Thomas Muirhead, who operated it as a private hotel. When the Muirheads retired in 1949, the hotel was run by Mr and Mrs Osborne Semple. A licence was granted in 1951.

Seven years later, in 1958, the property was acquired by Roxburgh County Council for use as a residential home for the elderly. However, it was closed by Scottish Borders Council in October 1995, most of the residents being transferred to Grove House, in Kelso. The Council then put Romany House up for sale.

One subsequent proposal by a potential purchaser was to convert Romany House into flats and to build a block of eight more units in the front garden, but following a public protest about these changes to a listed building, the proposal was withdrawn.

Romany House Hotel is again in private ownership.

Hatching and Despatching

In the early 1960s Yetholm was the scene of more than one enterprise involving the production and processing of chickens on a commercial scale. Kenneth Sibbald, a son of the late Mr William Sibbald, the grocer in Main Street, acquired the Old Brewery building about 1960, installed a large number of battery cages and went into egg production. He was living next door at Montgomerie Place. Then he turned the building into a chicken processing factory, despatching chickens with the aid of about ten employees, mostly women from the village. On the Loanings above the village until recently could be seen a 200 ft. chicken house, which Kenneth had built.

He also raised turkeys. In the hard winter of 1963, when there was deep snow for weeks on end, he had to walk the turkeys down from the Loanings, and thought himself fortunate to lose only 15 of the delicate birds. On one occasion he remembers lying in deep snow, exhausted and wanting to go to sleep, but aware that if he did, that would be fatal.

At one stage in his business he had birds housed at many different locations in and around Yetholm, mainly to minimise the risk of disease: he had so many birds that this attracted comment and some resistance.[1]

In the early 1960s the word "agri-business" was entering the language, and a Canadian company of international scope, Shaver Ltd., of Ontario, arrived in Yetholm. This came about after James Rutter Ltd., of Fulletby, Lincolnshire had obtained a Shaver franchise. Rutter's company, Northern Hatcheries

---

[1] Mr Kenneth Sibbald interviewed, 24 July 1999

Ltd., constructed a new building at the north end of Yetholm. This building, situated uphill from the primary school, is still there but was subsequently converted to a private dwelling, now belonging to Mr Douglas Gibson.

Kenneth Sibbald became a director of Northern Hatcheries. Shaver imported the parent stock from Sweden, and had selected breeding farms in various parts of Roxburghshire and Kirkcudbrightshire. There were two hatchings a week, each of 7,000 chicks. The professional veterinary consultant, incidentally, was Mrs Susan T. Smith, of Kelso, the sister of world champion racing driver Jim Clark.

It was one of the first franchised layer hatcheries in Scotland, and in 1966 became the exclusive Shaver distributor for Scotland and North-east England. Northern Hatcheries was sending day-old chicks by road to England, where they sold very easily – more easily than in Scotland, where rapid development of the industry had led to strenuous competition. Shaver headquarters in Canada bought eggs from Yetholm for many key export markets.

Kenneth remained with the company until 1964, when he left to concentrate on producing hatching eggs. In 1967 he went to South Africa, where he was engaged in the same industry, which was at a much earlier stage of commercial evolution. Kenneth was succeeded at Northern Hatcheries by Derek Cameron, who had returned to Yetholm not long before from Southern Rhodesia, where he had introduced "Chunky Chick" broiler stock. Derek was at Yetholm until late 1967, when he went to work as a technical director at Shaver headquarters in Canada.

During this time a number of well known residents worked in the Yetholm hatchery, including Albert Scott and his son, Allan. The hatchery foreman was David Borthwick. Lawrence Armstrong (father of the Scotland rugby player, Gary) and Eric Gilles did stints as drivers.

Much of the progress achieved by Shavers was due to the introduction of well-known Border farmers as hatching egg suppliers and pullet rearers. The outstanding hatchery supplier for all the Shaver operation was the late Mr Hall at Denholm, Mr Hall held all the production records among Shaver breeders. Production always peaked above 95 per cent and continued for months with hatchability over 98 per cent. Pullets reared on Mrs Hunter's farm at Ettrickbridge were always outstanding performers. Another top producer was the Pollock family, who built up their farm at Newbridge; their farm is still operating just off the roundabout next to the road to Edinburgh Airport.

The Yetholm hatchery was a regular exhibitor at the Royal Show at Stoneleigh. When Northern Hatcheries purchased a new delivery vehicle with a controlled environment, the vehicle was sent to the show that year with David Borthwick, so that he could spend most of the day driving up and down the traffic-jammed roads, making sure as many farmers as possible saw it. This publicity proved very profitable.

One interesting aspect of the chicken business in those days was that, while hatching eggs and chickens could be exported from Scotland to England, they were prohibited from coming the other way. The local policeman was very sharp on the issue, but Northern Hatcheries was never caught though occasionally questioned. However, some of their competitors thought that the "back road" from Wooler was an ideal way round the restriction. During the 1964 Highland Show at Edinburgh, Shaver staff suggested to the general manager of a major competitor that he should be careful about using that road because the local police might pick them up. The manager concerned strenuously denied any such contravention, but panicked considerably when Shaver presented him with his vehicles' registration numbers and movement times. Shaver did not want anyone to be caught, as that would have been bad for the whole industry.

Northern Hatcheries was bought by another company in late 1967, but as the swing to farmers buying brown egg layers accelerated, Shaver's lack of a first-class "brown bird" led to falling sales and the closure of the hatchery about 1971.

Ken Sibbald had spent his boyhood in Edinburgh and was evacuated to North Berwick during the Second World War. After leaving Kelso High School he worked for a grocer in Kelso for a year and then worked for six months with his father, Mr William Sibbald, who now had the former Hardie's grocery in Main Street, Yetholm. On being called up for National Service at 18, Ken served in the Korean War, where he was wounded. He returned to Yetholm in 1953. He was always fond of horses, and as a young man he gained experience of breaking horses from the late George Beveridge, who had the Plough Hotel from 1959 to 1969.

Chapter 11

The Twentieth Century

Advent of Motor Transport

In 1900 Sir George Douglas, of Kelso, went motoring with two friends in a Daimler. Later he reported: "In all we had travelled, roughly speaking, fifty miles, in something over five hours – a fair rate of progress, when ascents and adverse circumstances are taken into account.

"The cost of the four and a half gallons of petrol consumed on the way was five shillings and one penny three-farthings (London price); the number of travellers was three.... Horses seem already to be growing reconciled to the motor; at least, of those that we met on the road, very few did more than glance askance at it. Two years ago this was different." [1]

It is a vivid glimpse of the moment when the age of the horse was passing, giving way to the internal combustion engine, which was to change the world, and the lifestyle of Yetholm with it.

In the same year of 1900, however, there was still a horse-drawn carriage service between Yetholm and Kelso. It ran on Tuesdays and Fridays, twice a day; on Mondays, Wednesdays and Thursdays, once daily; and on Saturdays, three times. The single fare was one shilling, which was thought very dear. The same coach owner (Mr Mercer) would go to Mindrum railway station on request. The horse-drawn brake from Kelso carried the mail as well as holidaymakers, who sometimes found themselves seated on hampers of rabbits despatched by the local game dealer. The first motor-driven brake came to Yetholm just before the First World War, which broke out in August

[1] Sir George Douglas: *Diversions of a Country Gentleman* London 1902, pp144-153.

Travel in style: This splendid vehicle was owned by Mr Elliot of Clifton Park, Morebattle, and it has stopped at the Nichol cottage, near the south end of Town Yetholm. The date on the back of the photograph is 23 September 1909.

This early bus service, about to depart from the White Swan Hotel, Town Yetholm, probably linked the village with Kelso. The vehicle, which has solid tyres, may have been built before the First World War, but the clothing of the lady passenger suggests the early 1920s. The presence of the hotel owners on the doorstep (probably Mr and Mrs Andrew Robson) suggests a special occasion, perhaps an inaugural run.

1914. Ladies wore motoring veils over their hats, to protect their complexion from the wind. [2]

In 1930 someone in Yetholm, who evidently kept a close eye on what was going on, was sufficiently impressed to record that there were no fewer than 12 motor cars privately owned in the village, and about four motor cycles.

There were five bus runs to Kelso on weekdays, and seven on Saturdays, but no Sunday service. On weekdays there were two runs from Yetholm to Wooler, and two to Jedburgh. On Thursday nights there was a bus that took people to the cinema in Kelso. The special fare was 1s return, compared with the normal 2s 9d.

A newspaper advertisement of the time proclaimed that the motor bus "Gipsy Queen" ran daily to Kelso to meet trains – leaving Kirk Yetholm via the Plough Hotel at 8.45 a.m. and 12.45 p.m. Further details were obtainable from W.B. Whitelaw, Kirk Yetholm, by phoning Yetholm 3.[3]

Before the advent of the motor bus, the traditional annual outing known as the Spittal Trip recruited up to 20 highly decorated horse-drawn carts on the first Wednesday in July, to convey families to Mindrum railway station and thence to Spittal on the coast. It was a holiday for the whole village, and for many of those who took part it may have been their longest journey of the year. By about 1930 the trip was now made by motor charabanc, as many as ten vehicles being needed.

It was a steep rise in private car ownership, about a decade after the Second World War, that spelled the decline of public transport in rural areas, However, at that time the bus service from Yetholm was still sufficiently frequent that boys could travel in to the chip shop in Kelso for a multiple order and bring them back to the village piping hot for distribution!

By 1986, when the Rev. Joe Brown wrote a paper for the Third Statistical Account, he calculated that some 80 per cent of families and individuals in Yetholm owned motor cars, and almost 10 per cent owned more than one car.

---

[2] Isa Nichol: *Memories of Yetholm.*

[3] Mrs Jane Beveridge: *Yetholm Scrapbooks* 1958-1988.

Changed Days in Housing

The housing profile of Yetholm is an interesting mix. In the historic core of Town Yetholm, surrounding the green, the Victorian era dominates, interspersed with older cottages (one thatched); except at the summit of Dow Brae, the 20th century has been prevented from impinging upon the profile of the High Street.

Beyond this historic core, one encounters the occasional mansion, numerous houses built by the local authority, and a range of 20th century private development.

Many of the 18th century cottages were probably provided originally by the local landowners for their farm workers, many of whom had been moved into the village following the enclosure of outlying farm land and abandonment of ancient settlements, particularly in the Bowmont Valley.

In many cases, the tenancies of these new cottages included a right of grazing the family cow on the haugh, as well as entitlement to a smallholding or vegetable allotment on the patches of land known as the Loanings.

As time passed, however, and the local economy became less farming-oriented, cottages in both Town Yetholm and Kirk Yetholm were gradually sold by the landowners and the housing stock became increasingly owner-occupied. Government policy encouraged this trend.

In the Victorian period, better-off families had bought and demolished many of the cramped thatched cottages, with their massive walls and small windows, replacing them with more spacious, two-storey houses, featuring the characteristic dormer and bow windows.

Early photographs taken at the close of the 19th century offer useful clues about housing conditions in the village. It is important to remember that in those days housing expectations were lower. When one examines these fading photographs, the fabric of many of the cottages has a run-down look. Many of the houses in Town Yetholm and Kirk Yetholm had no running water; the supply had to be carried in pails from the street wells – interesting relics that have survived to this day as decorative street-furniture. Cottages in these old photos may look picturesque, but they were likely to be damp.

Between the two World Wars, there was already a trend towards home ownership and modernisation. More than one person, returning to Yetholm after an absence of many years, has commented: "The place looks so much tidier than I remember!"

Council housing in Yetholm was introduced between the Wars: probably the first examples were at Grafton Road, Town Yetholm in 1934. A prominent example of pre-war private housing development in the village are the houses at Nos 1-6 Morebattle Road, which were built by Fairnington of Branxton, Northumberland in 1932/33.

For a number of years after the Second World War, both villages had a number of "prefabs" – small prefabricated houses put up under a Government scheme to alleviate a severe post-war housing shortage. The small, sturdy prefabs became a part of British folklore and inspired an affectionate loyalty among their tenants, many of whom later moved out to bigger houses rather reluctantly. Woodbank Road, whose residents enjoy one of the finest outlooks in Yetholm, was built in three stages after the Second World War, beginning at the southern end of the street.

In the succeeding years, new-build housing in the private sector began to play an increasingly significant role in improvement of the housing stock.

Yetholm, as the only conservation village in Roxburghshire with a classification of "outstanding", enjoys special protection. More than 50 dwellings in the two villages are on the Secretary of State's list of buildings of special architectural or historic interest. Scottish Borders Council, like other local authorities and public agencies such as Historic Scotland, now weighs the value of restoration against demolition, and funds are available for the conservation of significant examples of vernacular Scottish architecture.

When Thatch Was King

Until the 19th century, all the cottages in Yetholm would have been roofed in thatch. This thatch would usually be of straw over a base of turf divots, but there are records of reed and heather being used, and probably rushes or bracken on some lesser buildings, for example the roofs of byres and other buildings accommodating animals.[1]

Only the very rich could afford to have slates, brought in by horse and cart over long distances and therefore at great expense.

Thatch in those days was the cheapest option for a number of reasons: the material could be obtained locally; you could use rough timbers on the roof; and to a large extent you could do it yourself. Labour was relatively cheap, though there was a lot of labour and time involved on a regular basis: one reason why thatched roofs lost favour was that labour became more expensive.

Thatch remained the cheap option until the coming of the railways in the mid-19th century, when it became possible to transport Welsh slate cheaply to this part of the country. So gradually slate roofs became standard throughout the Borders. Eventually thatched roofs became so rare that they acquired a curiosity value: they assumed a historical and cultural significance.

In Yetholm, historical photographs show that quite a number of thatched cottages survived into the 20th century. Today there is only a handful of

[1] In the 16th century, when the Earl of Hertford's punitive campaign put no fewer than 287 Border villages to the torch, it is said it was a fairly simple matter for the inhabitants to renew the thatched roofs on return from their temporary refuge in the hills.

thatched houses in the two Yetholms, and the most unusual of these is 18th century Myrtle Cottage in Town Yetholm, at the junction of Main Street and Yewtree Road.

The case is unusual in that its roof, having been converted about a century ago from thatch to slate, has reverted to thatch. The decision to put back a thatched roof was taken by the National Trust for Scotland under the Trust's Small Houses scheme. This work was carried out by a professional thatcher named Jeremy Cox, in 1995, and the house is now in private ownership.

The case of Myrtle Cottage is also interesting in that the building, though structurally sound, came close to being demolished because its position on a street corner was allegedly a hazard to traffic. The proposal to demolish was opposed on environmental grounds, and a public enquiry, held on the instructions of the Secretary of State for Scotland in 1992, found in favour of retaining the cottage.

As recently as the 1980s, the number of thatched houses in Scotland was rapidly diminishing. But since then there has been a revival of interest, and many local authority planners are thought to be sympathetic to thatch in appropriate circumstances – especially if it can be shown that there was a thatched roof on the building originally.

Thatch is perfectly good at keeping water out, if it is properly maintained. Regular maintenance is the key. Its life span depends on the materials used, but one can expect a roof made of reeds to last for 50 years before it requires some attention.

There are believed to be not more than half a dozen professional thatchers in Scotland today. Most of the reeds they use come from the banks of the River Tay. Scottish reeds are now exported to thatchers in England, where the durability of the local reeds is said to have been affected in some areas by chemicals used in modern farming.

Career of a Spymaster

On 22 January 1865 at Lochside, near Yetholm, there was born a man who was destined to rise to the highest rank in the Royal Navy This was Admiral of the Fleet Sir Henry Oliver, who lived on, in retirement in London, until the remarkable age of 101.

In mid-career, however, Sir Henry did attract some strenuously controversial views about his professional abilities. This occurred during the First World War, when he was in the post of Director of Naval Intelligence, to which he had been appointed in 1913.

The story has been dealt with by more than one historian of the British intelligence services.

Oliver, who seems to have been by nature a taciturn man, was given by his Senior Service colleagues the ambiguous nickname of "Dummy". One historian[1] concludes that Oliver, as Director of Naval Intelligence at the outbreak of war in 1914, did not know much about coding and decoding. To his credit, he quickly recruited someone who did. This was Sir Alfred Ewing, a fellow Scot who at the time was Director of Naval Education. Ewing was a former professor of engineering, and an expert in radio-telegraphy who had dabbled in codes and ciphers. His appointment led to the founding of the celebrated Room 40 at the Admiralty (which might be described as the prototype of the Second World War's decoding centre at Bletchley Park).

---

[1] Christopher Andrew: *Secret Service: The Making of the British Intelligence Community* London 1986 pp133-166.

The controversy about Sir Henry Oliver's abilities seems to stem from his reluctance to delegate. Christopher Andrew states that the conscientious Oliver, over worked, slept in the War Room at the Admiralty, hardly left it by day, and insisted on drafting personally all the signals based on the decoding effort of Room 40. This eventually led to Admiral Beatty, the celebrated commander of the Home Fleet, complaining that priceless information was being sat on at the Admiralty until it was too late for the forces at sea to take action. Oliver, it was said, despite a capacity for intolerable workloads, could not possibly find time during a great naval battle (Jutland, in May 1916, was cited as an example) to interpret personally all the decrypts from Room 40.

Oliver was succeeded as DNI about November 1914 by a more famous spy-master, Admiral Reginald ("Blinker") Hall but remained in a supervisory post attached to Room 40. From 1920 until 1924 he was Second Sea Lord; became an Admiral in 1923; and Admiral of the Fleet in 1928, in which year he was created GCB. In 1933 he went on the retired list, but in 1940, following the outbreak of the Second World War, was restored to the active list at the age of 75. After the war Sir Henry visited his birthplace, and was fishing on Yetholm Loch when in his nineties.

The historians tell one further remarkable story of the cloak-and-dagger variety. It became known as the Alexander Szek case. In German-occupied Brussels in 1915, Szek evidently gained access to a German diplomatic cipher. The British were eager to acquire the cipher, but negotiations were unfruitful and Szek suddenly died in rather mysterious circumstances. Many years later, when he was in his eighties, Sir Henry Oliver, interviewed by historian Stephen Roskill[2], said more than once: "I paid £1,000 to have that man shot."

Christopher Andrew also attributes to Sir Henry a remark that is an espionage truism: "In this underground business" he said "there is always a danger of being double-crossed."

---

[2] Alan Judd: *The Quest for C* London 2000, p.365.

Hard Winters

There were four memorably hard winters in Yetholm during the 20th century – in 1941, 1947, 1963 and 1969. By common consent the hardest of these was 1963, not only because of heavy snowfalls in blizzard conditions, but also because of the length of time the snow remained.

The storm started on Christmas Day 1962, and the thaw did not set in until 6 March. In the main street of Yetholm at one stage, the snow lay almost two feet deep, and the snowdrifts on the roads to Halterburn, Morebattle, Mindrum and Kelso were deeper than anyone could remember. Yetholm was virtually cut off from the world.

Border newspapers recorded the event in detail. Up at Sourhope, drifts of 14 feet were measured. In Yetholm, someone measured an icicle 8 ft 4 in long. One newspaper photograph showed shepherd George Scott and two others, accompanied by Mr Scott's collie dog, walking along the roof of the byre at Mainside: at one stage the byre had been completely covered.

But the drifting snow did not keep 15-year-old Jim McGregor, of Halterburn, from attending Kelso High School. He walked two miles over the fields to join the school bus.

As the days lengthened into weeks, snowploughs were overwhelmed, and broke down. Train services were cancelled between Kelso and Berwick. All bus services out of Kelso were cancelled.

The outlying farms were worst off, with shepherds struggling in near impossible conditions to dig out sheep, and carrying fodder on their backs to keep their flocks alive.

In February, though there was a general thaw elsewhere in the country, many homesteads in the rural areas continued to be immersed in deep snow. In the Kalewater and Bowmont valleys, drifting snow and blocked roads caused chaos, and as the weeks passed there was growing criticism by outbye farmers of the County Council's marathon efforts to cope.

One roads foreman said the task of clearing snow from side roads was the worst in his 36 years' experience. He remembered the blizzard of 1947 but reckoned that in the latest emergency the fall of snow had been much heavier, with many more roads blocked.

Lighting the Streets

The streets were lit by paraffin lamps from about 1930, and were not replaced by electric lamps until after the Second World War. The paraffin street lamps were looked after by Charlie Douglas, who was also employed by the County Council as the village dustman.

Charlie and his refuse barrow were a familiar sight, as he kept the cobbled gutters clear of weeds with a narrow hoe, swept the streets and took the rubbish down to the village tip, which was at the foot of Dow Brae.

Every evening, with his ladder, he climbed to each street lamp in turn, withdrew the paraffin holder, filled it if necessary and lit the lamp. At 10 p.m. every evening he returned, climbed to each lamp and turned out the light. He did this for years.

Mischievous boys were in the habit, while Charlie was up the ladder, of lifting the base of the ladder off the gound and shaking it, despite Charlie's protests.

Professor John Gray

John Gray was one of Yetholm's most famous sons, much loved and held in great regard. Retired to Kelso after a life of scholarship, he was often seen wandering around his birthplace, "Dear Old Kirk Yetholm", meeting old friends and making new, whom he regaled with nostalgic stories of his boyhood and the characters of that time in Kirk Yetholm.

Very much the true Borderer, John was most proud of his origin. He contrasted the peace and quiet in Yetholm of the present day, which he described "as that of an eventide home", with the "stir and excitement of the gypsy metropolis" of his youth in the 1920's.

For much of his youth John lived at "The Cross Keys" in Kirk Yetholm, which had been an inn and is now a guest house.

The work of the village in those days was mainly buying and selling; most families were merchants with horse and cart. They dealt in pots, rabbits, young pigs, broken wool, and "clerts", which John described as "sheep's wool clotted with dung which were cut from the sheep's buttocks, bought from the shepherds for a small sum, washed and sold to the tweed mills in Jedburgh".

John had a great liking for the nicknames of the Yetholm characters of his day. Amongst these were "Potty Mary" so named after her merchandise; Bob Robson "The Bumper" who drove his wife "Nellie" about hawking drapery; "Stovie Jock" who sold hardware, mainly pot lids; and Jockie Stenhouse "The Pinter".

Many were the stories John would tell about these characters and others whom he could recall with great clarity.

We are indebted to *The Scots Magazine* for some of these details and to Colin MacDermott, Executive Editor of *The Herald* and William Johnstone for the following obituary which best describes the varied and rich life and achievement of John Gray.

The Rev Professor John Gray MA, BD, PhD, DD
Professor of Hebrew and Semitic Languages, University of Aberdeen
Born 9 June 1913 and died 1 April 2000

John Gray was born and brought up in Kirk Yetholm, high in the Cheviots, the older son of a master tailor. He had that particular quality of Scottish patriotism that only one reared so near the Border could possess.

From his childhood and youth in those rural surroundings he imbibed those virtues of a countryman's independence and self-sufficency that marked him to the end of his days; the skilled fisherman that could tie his own flies and had that intuitive knowledge of weather and light and water conditions to go out of an evening and, as he would put it , "fill a basket"; the beekeeper (on his retirement from Aberdeen he transported his hives in the removal van back to his native Kelso and received from the enraged bees 150 stings for his pains); the gardener, and really in his early days, smallholder and crofter, who, when in his isolated manse in Arran he was snowed up for six weeks, was perfectly able to support himself and his growing family; the piper and fiddler, devotee of Scott Skinner.

He often said that if he had not become a minister and then an academic he would have been a Border shepherd. But he was quickly marked out as the proverbial Scottish "lad o' pairts". Proceeding to Edinburgh University, he took a First in Classics, followed by a BD with Distinction in Old Testament. En route, he took time to study Arabic with Richard Bell, the renowned interpreter of the Koran; as Blackie Scholar, he spent a year travelling in Greece and the Holy Land.

It was on that journey that in the famed Dominican Ecole he had, as he would say, the newly discovered Ras Shama texts put in his hands, which were to stand in the forefront of his research in a lifetime of academic endeavour. Ordained as a missionary in Haifa with the Church of Scotland in the fateful year of 1939, he returned to the Holy Land as Chaplain to the Palestine Police. This experience gave him opportunity to travel the length and breadth of

John Gray as a young graduate

the land, to accumulate an unrivalled knowledge of its landscape and its topography and an intimate acquaintance with the life and manners of its inhabitants, especially the Arabs. He would , like the true countryman he was, "disappear for days into the desert with the Bedouin". Thus he acquired at first hand those anthropological observations that he would later effectively deploy in his writings; for that experience too he had prepared while still a Divinity student by study at Greifswald under the Palestinian anthropologist Gustav Dalman.

He returned to Scotland at the end of 1941 by Norwegian ship. Gifted linguist that he was, Gray did not let the opportunity slip of learning Norwegian, an unbelievable feat, even if the return route was by the Cape, but confirmed many years later he was, to his profound satisfaction, invited to give two lectures founded in memory of his most admired mentor, Sigmund Mowinckel in Oslo. Gray determined to deliver his lectures in Norwegian. He had his manuscript checked by the Head of the Scandinavian Studies in the University of Aberdeen, who pronounced the Norwegian excellent, if somewhat marred by nautical slang.

Back in Scotland, he was inducted in 1942 to the Parish of Kilmory on the Island of Arran. In that remote setting, he set himself to prepare for a life in academe. The Ugaritic texts he had first met in Ecole Biblique, and which were still in the early days of interpretation, he subjected to fundamental study; in their elucidation he found in Arabic "the golden key" (during that period he also read through the whole of the Koran in Arabic).

An opening in Semitic Languages in Manchester under the redoubtable H H Rowley offered itself in 1947; there he once again found himself in the company not just of Old Testament scholars but of Arabists and anthropologists. Half-a-dozen years later a lectureship in Hebrew and Semitic languages became available in Aberdeen and to Aberdeen he came, where he was to spend the rest of his active academic life, first as Lecturer (1953-62), then as Professor (1962-80). While Gray was willing to take his share of administrative duties (he served as Dean of the Faculty of Divinity for a three-year period), his first love was undoubtedly research. He wrote voluminously in several areas. On Ugaritic, he produced an edition of the Keret Text (1955), a comprehensive study of the then known corpus of texts in the Legacy of Canaan (1957), both published by the prestigious academic house Brill, and at a more popular level, The Canaanites (1964) and Near Eastern Mythology (1969).

In archaeology, he wrote a volume Archaeology and the Old Testament World (1962) and a History of Jerusalem (1969). On the Old Testament he published commentaries on the historical books, Joshua, Judges and Ruth (1967), and on Kings (1964). But in Old Testament studies his first love was Psalms; there he sought to complement Mowinckel's "cult functional" approach developed in the 1920's with the insights newly garnered from the Ugaritic texts; this work came to fruition in his theological study, The Biblical Doctrine of the Reign of God (1979).

In this busy and productive academic career he took only one year off, to be visiting Professor at McMaster University, Hamilton, Ontario, in 1972. Public recognition of his scholarly contribution was given through the conferment on him of the honorary degree of DD by the University of St Andrews in 1977. Throughout his retirement Gray continued to work on another poetic corpus, the book of Job (which he had once rendered in the Doric, "Job in a Cheviot plaid"), returning again to Arabic and Ugaritic as principal means of elucidating its obscurities.

A colleague in another university once referred to him as "an old-fashioned Scottish professor". That is indeed a compliment that well sums up John Gray; the immense erudition, the single-minded dedication to long hours in the study, the impact of that learning and industry on his students, and the response of affection and respect that he elicited from them by his transparent quality and utter genuineness as a scholar and as a personality.

It is indeed hard to see how his like can be produced again.

William Johnstone

William Johnstone, *The Herald*, Tuesday, April 25, 2000. Obituary for Rev Professor John Gray, MA, BD, PhD, DD.

John Gray "Dear Old Kirk Yetholm" *The Scots Magazine*, February 1962.

John Gray "The Man from Bowmont Water" *The Scots Magazine*, February 1973.

Tibbie Herbert

Indefatigable is a word that springs to mind in describing Miss Tibbie Herbert. Her name remains celebrated for the prodigious range of service, mostly voluntary, which she gave to Yetholm as an administrator over a period of more than 40 years.

Again and again Miss Isobel Herbert's name is encountered as one researches some of the traditional organisations in the village. When any new communal project was being mooted, Tibbie was the person the organisers first thought of when looking for an administrator. Perhaps the best way of telling her story is to quote from a newspaper interview which she gave at her home, Deanfield, in February 1968.

Tibbie's father, who was a local builder, had been the village registrar, and on his death about 1941 Tibbie succeeded him in the post. She also became clerk to Roxburghshire School Management Committee. Tibbie was the founder secretary of Yetholm Unionist Association from 1947 until 1956, and secretary of Yetholm W.R.I. until her retirement in 1967. She remained secretary of the Wauchope Hall, looking to its maintenance and being responsible for letting the premises. She was also honorary secretary of Yetholm Horticultural Society. In 1946 she became secretary of Yetholm Border Shepherds' Show and was the leading organiser of this annual event. She was the secretary of the Joint Sports Committee, which administered the upkeep of the village playing field and ran the annual sports festival.

For at least 20 years Tibbie also organised the annual visit of the Kelso Laddie. She was also the village librarian and worked in the library three evenings a week. For her services to the community, Tibbie was awarded the M.B.E.

A Light Celebration

The introduction of street lighting in Kirk Yetholm (or a welcome improvement of it) was celebrated in verse by a village poet, who signed his work, "Jagger Jock".

These were paraffin-oil lamps, which were lit every evening by a well-known village employee, Charlie Douglas: the poet expresses gratitude to Charlie in the final verse.

The verses are interesting for a number of reasons. There is an oblique reference to the traditional rivalry with Town Yetholm, which appears to have installed street lighting at an earlier date.

A careful reading of the poem reveals a number of vantage points in Kirk Yetholm at which the new lamps have been placed to everyone's benefit (at the Green; the Cross Keys; Yetholm Mill; the manse; and the bridge over the Bowmont). The poet marvels that it is now possible to draw water at a street well at night. Progress, indeed!

Lastly, the poem is interesting because it incorporates a good few Romany words, which even then must have been passing from common use, for a glossary is appended.

Kirk Yetholm Lights

The nicht before December came
Kirk Yetholm gleamed wi' licht
That ancient spot o' gypsy fame
Became a modern sicht.

Lichts here an' there met human eye
A' roond the village ways
Hark! shade o' Esther seems to sigh
No' like my by-gane days.

Oor neebors 'cross the Bowmont stream
Are kittle e'en tae titter
When lichts owre there gi'e sic a gleam
Oh! That's just goosey-gander.

They wha thole best gey aften win
An' patience brings fair due
For equal richts are ne'er a sin
Kirk Yetholm's proved that true.

Sic mangin owre the tikne things
Wad tak' a peck o' varro
Tae wipe the tchibs o' ill-faured bings
That cry bing lay your shero.

Doon by the clapin stands a licht
There's ane for canghri patre
Johnnie's taft is e'er sae bricht
Though a' cost barre louer.

The knight of old, respeckkit too
Has ane tae licht his way;
Hooray! The Cross Keys corner view
Is noo as licht as day.

When comin' frae the toon at nicht
An' thro' the Haugh ye roam
Ye'll find ane near the brig alicht
Tae guide ye safely home.

The auld Green has its beam nae doot
Tae guide douce dwellers there
Across the sward or roond aboot
Gosh! man, that is gey fair.

If peevan you wid want tae gae
A licht shines brichtly forth
On keir, an' a' folks seem tae say
For motors it's much worth.

Brave Staerough's way is no' let want
For boldly stands a lowe;
Folks can get pawne at the pant
In darkness noo I trow.

Noo last o' a' oor brave gadge
Is gallant barre Chairlie
Wha lichts the lamps wi' hearty glee
Ne'er feart, be't late or airly.

"Jagger Jock"

Mangin – *speaking*
Tikne – *insignificant*
Varro – *meal*
Tchibs – *tongues*
Bings – *Deils*
Bing lay your shero – *an evil wish*
Clapin – *mill*
Canghri patre – *Church minister*
Barre - *bonny*
Barre louer – *good money*
Peevan – *drinking*
Keir – *house*
Pawne – *water*
Pant – *pump*
Gadge – *man*

In verse 10, the puzzling word "motors" may be a misprint for "mouters", i.e. the Scots word for multures, a fee (for grinding grain): the poet is saying that the street lighting is worth the money.

The Youth Hall

The building we now know as the Youth Hall has played a variety of useful roles in its history, which can be traced back to the 18th century.

It is believed that one of its earliest uses, almost 250 years ago, was as a weavers' shed. At that time weaving was still a cottage industry, and it is possible there was more than one loom in the building. But the weave from the loom probably proceeded, like others in Town Yetholm and Kirk Yetholm, to Blunty's Mill for further processing.

Later, at some stage, it is believed the building was used as a stable. Then, in 19th century maps, the building is identified as the "Town Hall". It is unlikely to have been a Town Hall in the sense of the centre of municipal administration: rather it was probably the only community meeting-place in the village at that time.

In the 1930s, the building was employed by the Young Men's Christian Association (YMCA) as a social club. Like other "YM" clubs throughout the United Kingdom, it was also known as the "Red Triangle Club" because of its distinctive logo. The club in Yetholm was founded by Mr Alfred (Bob) Daw, father of Arthur and Webb Daw. The facilities offered by the club, not only to village members but members of the YMCA passing through, included a reading room, writing facilities, music, refreshments, a games room with two full-size billiard tables, table tennis, carpet bowls and darts. Visiting members were also offered baths, presumably at the homes of local members.

In the post-war years it became the headquarters of a Boy Scout troop (the troop earlier had used the Good Templars' Hall nearby and the Old Brewery) and the Girl Guides. It also for a time was the home of a village youth club.

In 2000, following renovation and financial support from National Lottery funds, the building began a fresh chapter in its history of service to the community, complementing the much larger Wauchope Hall by providing valuable accommodation for meetings of smaller groups.

The renovation was carried out at an initial cost of £24,000: the funding came from village events and grants from a number of bodies, including the National Lottery (Awards for All), Scottish Community Foundation, Scottish Borders Council and Yetholm Community Council.

Yetholm at War

Sixty years after the event, Bessie Martin vividly recalled standing one night on the family farm, at Thornington, Mindrum, watching the fields engulfed in flames. This dramatic scene occurred about 1941. The crops had been set alight by incendiary bombs, unloaded by German bombers. The aircraft were returning from a raid on west Scotland, and were dumping the hazardous surplus before crossing the North Sea to land at their home airfield in occupied Norway.

This spectacular incident, which incidentally ruined the blackout that night, was one of many abnormal events experienced by civilians in the rural Borders, on what was called the "Home Front", during the Second World War. Bessie moved to Yetholm with her parents in 1943.

Yetholm's playing field, today a tranquil corner of the village, was at one point in the war an Army searchlight battery, its two powerful generators dispersed for safety from possible attack along the Cherrytrees road and the Mindrum road.

For a time the playing field was a prisoner of war camp, or it may possibly have been a camp for interned seafarers whose ships had been intercepted in the North Sea. The internees were housed in wooden huts on brick foundations, alongside a toilet and shower block. Camouflage netting and traces of barbed wire fencing can still be found in the long grass.

If it was indeed a camp for prisoners of war, the coils of barbed wire do not seem to have been very effective: it is said that prisoners would creep out at night and gather a few potatoes from an adjacent field. Carefully restoring the disturbed drills, they returned to the camp and made homemade schnapps.

Another story concerns German prisoners who were sent out each day to work on local farms, escorted by a middle aged but nonetheless armed member of the Pioneer Corps. On one occasion, on walking to Primside, they were told by the farmer that there was no work that day because of the poor weather. The soldier from the Pioneer Corps was very tired, and on the return walk to Yetholm it was noticed that one of the Germans was carrying the soldier's rifle for him. The war must have seemed a long way off that day.

Nationally there was a great drive to grow more food, including the cultivation of borderline hill land which in normal times would not have been considered economic. Petrol rationing curtailed travel, and there was relatively little traffic on the roads. Many motorists laid up their cars for the duration.

The YMCA Club (now the Youth Hall) was used by the Army for recreation: the club's facilities, particularly the billiard table and the table tennis, were very popular. The sergeants' mess was a few doors along from Hardie's the grocer, and the officers' mess was at Hall House. The Mission Hall provided accommodation for soldiers.

There was a Polish Army brigade encamped between Yetholm and Kelso. Their training ranged across the local countryside, and one of their Bren gun carriers, in attempting to negotiate Dodds' Vennel at speed, collided with Jim Dodds' house.

RAMC officers billeted in the village were on their way to the Far East. As in all other communities, the war led to wide ranging social disruption, whose effects were to prove permanent. Men and women in Yetholm were called up or volunteered to serve in the Forces, or moved away to other war work in factories.

On the walls of the Wauchope Hall are two rolls of honour, each bearing the names of about 100 individuals. One lists those from Yetholm who served in the First World War, and the other those in the Second World War. Those who died for their country are identified: mercifully the number was much lower in the 1939-45 conflict, as the war memorial at Mill Brae, Kirk Yetholm confirms.

The R.A.F. flew regular training flights over the Cheviots, and there were a number of fatal crashes in the hills: those killed included not only British but other Allied aircrew. There were German dead, too, recovered from the wreck of a Heinkel bomber.

Every civilian was issued with a National Identity Card. Evacuee children appeared at Yetholm Primary School. Everything was either rationed or in short supply, from oranges to No 8 torch batteries. There was no television, and a radio set, often battery-operated, was a virtual necessity to remain informed.

Housewives were "registered customers" with a retailer of their choice. White flour became a rarity, being replaced by National Flour, which was almost brown but not quite. Items sold discreetly "under the counter" were a treat. Clothing coupons were treasured; a girl engaged to be married gratefully accepted gifts of clothing coupons from her relatives. Food rationing continued for up to nine years after the war ended (bread rationing was not introduced until 1946 and lasted for two years).

During the war there were many more vegetable allotments in Yetholm – not only along Yewtree Road, which was still open land as far as the "Goat", but also at the foot of the village. There were regulations governing everything: if you kept chickens, your egg ration was withheld. Butchers could not slaughter an animal unless it was injured. Occasionally, on the quiet, a pig would be shot dead with a .22 rifle and then have its leg broken to comply with the law. And relatives living in the big cities would turn up in Yetholm for a family visit, well aware that rationing in rural areas made country menus slightly less constrained.

Chapter 12

Personal Recollections

Memories of Yetholm

by Isa Nichol

Isa Nichol, who died in 1964 aged 58 years, composed an affectionate memoir of her life in Yetholm, spanning 50 years. It provides a personal and unique glimpse of a way of life that had changed greatly during her lifetime. She touches on changes in farm work, housing, shops, transport, school, churchgoing, and the welfare system, as well as village traditions and customs. It is a fascinating picture of a close–knit and relatively isolated community.

Very little is known of the circumstances in which the text was created. It may be that her memories were handwritten in the first instance, though no manuscript version is known. Perhaps they were delivered verbally in the course of conversation with a friend–cum–local historian. At some point the text was typed, either by Isa or a friend, admittedly not very expertly, on an elderly manual typewriter. A typed text inYetholm History Society's archive has the appearance of one of several copies made on an old–style duplicator. The memoir is published here for the first time.

Mrs Isobel Storie, whose selfless voluntary work on behalf of other villagers is warmly praised in the memoir, lived in a cottage (now gone) on the corner of Main Street and Dow Brae. This additional information about Mrs Storie was provided by her grand–daughter, who resides in Whitley Bay, and who visited the Society's 1996 exhibition, "A Century of Change" in the Stable Gallery.

Amongst the Cheviot hills there lies a village by the name of Yetholm. The old spelling was Yetham, meaning gate village or the hamlet with the gate. Whether it meant the first village in Scotland that is over the border from England, or the village with the toll–gate, I don't know.

At one time there were four toll houses, all of which are still standing. Two are in disuse, the other two are still inhabited, one going by the appropriate name of Catch–a–Penny. I knew an old lady who remembered that toll–gate in the time of horse drawn carriages when toll was paid and the fun they had bolting past the gate–keeper in an effort to beat the tax.[1]

There are two villages, one Kirk–Yetholm, the other Town Yetholm, the Bowmont Water flows between the two. Kirk–Yetholm is by tradition a Gipsy settlement, though no real gipsies live there now. Inter–marriage and a more modern way of life has changed all that.

Town–Yetholm – whoever named it 'Town' perhaps foresaw a time when it really would be a town, and in the not too distant future it will be just that, as it is growing every year, though to us old Yetholm folk that will be a sad day. The old friendly ways are going and old customs dying out.

Town–Yetholm and the surrounding lands were owned by the Wauchopes of Niddrie. Some of the land has been sold, and most of the old houses are owned by the tenants, people who have come to the village and bought them up, only a few are in Wauchope's name now.

The first Wauchope 'Laird' was General Wauchope, he was greatly revered by the people of the village. Many a time in my youth I've heard it said "Had the General been alive Yetholm would be a different place." It was he who put in our first water scheme, free of charge, the village didn't pay water rate for two generations. He was always making improvements. He also cared for the poor and the aged so far as he was able. Coal came from the Niddrie coalfields each winter to warm many a poor soul in need, the widow and the fatherless were never forgotten. When the General was killed at Magersfontein in the South African War, the village mourned him deeply, so much so, that they erected a memorial to his memory. It stands on the green and always goes by the name of 'the Monument'. I can remember the time when nearly every house had a picture or photo of the 'General' as he was affectionately called. It was always given a place of honour in the home.

Yetholm is purely agriculture and always has been, a few of the small farms were mills, they milled the oats for oatmeal, the larger farm owners bringing their oats to be milled. The mills are now in disuse, only the names remain

[1] No doubt people did try on occasion to evade payment at toll–gates, but evidently not at Catch–a–penny: as is explained elsewhere in this book, Catch–a–Penny seems to have been a smithy, not a toll house.

– Primside Mill, Duncanhaugh Mill, Yetholm Mill etc. There were several breweries too,[2] one in the haugh of which nothing remains but the name – 'Malt barns' better known now–a–days as Matt barns, there's still an old building in the middle of the village which goes by the name of the Brewery.

Blunty's Mill was a blanket mill, it still made blankets in my youth, but the owner died and the mill lade was done away with, so now we have no blanket mill though the old building still stands, and the two houses of the owners which went by the name of 'The Crescent' but now is 'Waukford'.

I can remember three churches in the parish, the United Presbyterian, the Free, after the union with the U.P. the United Free, and the established Church of Scotland, all were faithfully attended. People walking over the hills for miles or coming in carts. Shepherds even bringing their dogs. The U.P. and the Free were united in 1914. Mrs Wauchope bought the U.P. and gave it to the village [in 1919] and it is now known as the Wauchope Hall. The U. Free and the Established were united in 1940.

The Established is in Kirk–Yetholm and is a lovely building. Built of local whinstone quarried from 'Staerough', the hill behind the village, the stones all hand cut and built by Mr Herbert the local mason and builder at that time. He also built the bridge over the Bowmont between the villages. It says a lot for his skill as the bridge remained in the floods of 1948 when many another was washed away.

The hill next to Staerough – Coldsmouth on the map, but known locally as Cout's Nowt (if that's how you spell it) meaning goat's skin – a ship of gold was said to have been buried there. There were excavations there some years ago but whether anything was found I don't know. From the top of Cout's Nowt the formation of a Roman fort[3] can be seen. Between Cout's Nowt and Staerough there is the common where sheep were grazed, and behind Staerough there is the farm of Halterburn.

I read in an old book that there was once an Abbey there, the monks were shepherds. It is certainly a delectable spot for an Abbey, for walking in the valley there you can feel the peace and the stillness of God. Truly you can

---

[2] Isa's surprising statement that there were "several breweries" in Yetholm may be explained by the fact that at one time beer was brewed on individual farms, usually by the farmer's wife.

[3] An Iron Age fort? Both Green Humbleton and the Rings Plantation above Kirk Yetholm are possible locations.

sing there "I to the hills will lift mine eyes". Whether the Abbey story is legend or not, Halterburn House is incorporated with some remaining walls of an older building.[4]

Venchen Hill has a 'virtue well' now alas with the water cut off and over grown with weeds till you can hardly see it. It is surrounded by a grove of trees, there used to be twenty or more different species, though many have been cut down by now.

Our old schoolmaster used to take us to see it, and we had to name them all. A practical nature study lesson. Looking back I think our schoolmaster must have been an exceptional person. Besides giving us the three R's he had to give classes in woodwork, singing, and P.T. He was also Registrar and Poor Inspector, that is, he had to visit those who got 'off the parish'. No dole or National Assistance those days, to get 5/– was a King's ransom, but many a widow did without, bringing up her family as best she could.

I knew one who took what she called double work in the fields, that was doing two shifts instead of one, with her youngest child dumped somewhere near her, for want of a better place to put her. Another who brought up her family by working fields herself, keeping a cow, and garden for produce, yet that same person was the unofficial district nurse. If anybody was ill it was 'Send for Mrs Storie.' If anybody died it was 'Send for Mrs Storie' and she must have helped to bring countless babies into the world. She had no hospital training nor any degree in nursing. Just her own good sense and her willingness to help. Anytime of the day or night she could always be called on, and the medical profession did not frown on her. She even helped to bring the Doctor's bairns into the world. She was an old lady who I remember had a kindly word and a cheery countenance at all times. She hadn't much as regards this world's goods, but she gave of the things that she had, but not for money, for I never heard she got payment. She was a real neighbour and a friend indeed. To–day we have a District Nurse, but there are some things she's not allowed to do that Mrs Storie did out of a kindly heart.

Visitors to Yetholm were amused and often annoyed with the cow horn which the cow herd blew at 6 a.m. when all holiday makers expect to be sound asleep. There were usually about 14 cows and they grazed on the haugh in summer. A boy of about 14 years just left school was employed to call them out, and watch them during the day and call them in at night. The cows all

---

[4] Kelso Abbey had grazing rights at Shotton, possibly extending up the Halter Burn. So these may have been Abbey lands.

knew the horn and answered to it, leaving their respective byres, wending their way to the haugh. The same on the return journey, each branching off when they came near their own byre.

One old lady disdained the Haugh and took Betty her cow to her own field, leading her by halter. It was a sight to see, she leading Betty, and her sister coming behind with two of Betty's calves. When she got too old to keep a cow, she sold Betty to the local butcher, but she did not visit the butcher for a month in case she got a bit of Betty. Alas the village cows have been driven from the byres by modern regulations and we now get our milk in bottles, though to my mind it doesn't taste half as good.

In the old days we got lots of summer visitors, about every other house took in lodgers. They were looked forward to by the shop keepers and the village folk. The same visitors came year after year and became friends. It must have been an adventure getting here as transport wasn't too good, and our nearest railway was miles away.[5]

I remember the horse drawn brake which went to Kelso once a day. Anybody coming off the later train had to be content with a ride on the mail gig, which wasn't a mail gig at all but was owned and driven by a game dealer who obliged by bringing the mail, so passengers had to share their seat with baskets of rabbits or should I say hampers, and sometimes even had to sit on the said hampers. Perhaps it was all part of the holidays, along with washing themselves with rainwater etc.

Our first motor–driven brake came just before the first World War. It was just like a brake only without horses. It was then ladies used motoring veils over their hats, when they ventured to Kelso. Now when we see buses running six times a day, looking back it seems a different world, but there was something nice about those days, a community spirit and a friendly atmosphere that seems lacking today.

People are filled with apprehension. Two World Wars have done that, there is no longer tranquillity and peace of mind. Some things have been for the better, transport opening up the country and indeed other lands. Medical science and many more new inventions for the good of mankind, yet there are many for destruction too, that men's hearts and minds are failing them.

---

[5] Tourism is not a 20th century invention. Tourism had its roots in the development of the railways in the 19th century. Lots of people came to Yetholm for their holidays. They came either from the east coast line to Mindrum Station or by rail to Kelso. In both cases the final stage of the journey was by horse drawn brake.]

Would that we could get back that measure of peacefulness and trust that our forefathers had. That good would ultimately triumph and in the words of Rabbie Burns 'That man to man the world o'er would brithers be'.

In many ways our village was more or less self–supporting. We had joiners, blacksmiths, saddler, shoemakers, a watchmaker, tailors, dressmakers, Post Office and all the food shops essential to a community. Now there are very few trades left. The blacksmith and saddler have made way for the garage. Joiners carry on but in a different way. Bread comes from a distance, and though there are grocers and a butcher, we are largely served by the travelling shops.

The school is now a Primary School, the older children taken by bus to Morebattle or Kelso. No long walks to school now, and a teacher comes to give them P.T. so what they lose on the swings they gain on the roundabouts as it were.

We had our bad times between the two Wars. Yes, unemployment was rife here too. Farmers tended to rear cattle and sheep instead of crops, as they are doing now, and it was the beginning of the mechanical age, needing fewer workers on the land. Many a young lad never had regular employment until he was called to the forces in 1939. We were all poor then, it wasn't a case of 'keeping up with the Jones' but how to keep going at all.

We had three events in the year – Fastern E'en, Spittal Trip, and the 'Show'. Fastern E'en was a sports day, starting about 10 a.m. with a band of sorts. Someone carrying a banner with 'Let Yetholm Flourish' on it, followed by a drummer and anybody else who liked to take part. Sports were held on that bit of the haugh called the Beat. Then after 4 p.m. there was the ball game between single and married men. As far as I can remember it was who could get it into the Bowmont Water first. The ball was made of leather by the local shoemaker or cobbler as he was called. His wife dressed it up in ribbons. It was then taken from door to door and a collection taken, presumably to pay for the prizes. At 4 p.m. it was presented to the oldest inhabitant who kicked it off into the melee of young men who were waiting for it. Then ensued a lively and boisterous game. Many are the tales of duckings and mishaps but all was done in fun. This event was stopped during the 1914–1918 War, and revived again after the War ended, but people had lost interest so it wasn't continued.

Spittal Trip was another great day in the year, the first Wednesday in July, when all the village was on holiday. Farm carts were brought out, all were spick and span, and the horses' harness shining and decked off with ribbons and coloured wool. These took us to Mindrum, the nearest railway station four miles away where we got the train to Tweedmouth. Then we had to walk to Spittal. The one and only time we saw the sea in the whole year, so it was a red letter day. Now we can get any day to Spittal, and though Spittal Trip is still held, it has lost some of its magic.

The 'Show' is the first Saturday in October. It started I believe in a small way with only sheep. It was a Shepherds' Show, and still goes under that name, but now it is Industrial as well as having sports. It is still a great day, and a local get–together for farm and country folk alike.

Looking back over 50 years, it is as though we are in a different world now. But not so. It was the horse–driven era that gave us the motor car, it was the motor era that gave us the aeroplane, and it's the aeroplane era that is now giving us space–ships. It's the past that makes the present and the present the future. In the words of the poet, E.A. Guest:

All the countless thousand ages,
Lost or kept in History's pages
Lit the torch or paved the way
For the world we have today.

Whether Soldier, sage or peasant
We who make the living present
Are the past and just as they
For the future pave the way.

Had some ancient Hero faltered,
Or his course one footstep altered
By that difference long ago
Different were the life we know.

Time in us is endless, deathless
Breathing now, or sleeping breathless
Of the first and of the last
We are present, future, past.

Boyhood Memories

by Tom Smith

Tom Smith, of Kirk Yetholm, who died on 28 November 1997, aged 79, was a delightful man and an enthusiastic supporter of Yetholm History Society. Not long before he died he was persuaded to set down on paper his memories of happy boyhood, family and early working days. In the Second World War, as a soldier, Tom miraculously survived fierce fighting in North–West Germany, 1944–45; he was subsequently interviewed for a video commissioned by the Imperial War Museum.

It would appear that the older we grow, the more vivid our memory becomes of that wonderful period of boyhood, in a very happy family home in this delightful village. Starting when I first went to school in 1923, escorted by my elder sister, with strict instruction from Mother to behave, and listen to everything the teacher told us. This time must have been after the summer holidays. I was handed over to the teacher, who seated Adam Wyllie and myself at a desk for two, in the front row. This is the sum total of my memory of the first day at school.

Adam Wyllie and myself were very close friends all our school days, unfortunately Adam died in his early teen years.

We did learn to write, on framed slates with a round slate pencil, a practice that continued all my school days, hence the reason I have no written records of progress of any kind. But I can remember that I very seldom got into trouble with school work. However, the playground was a different story. The rough and tumble of playtimes was a very vast change from the sheltered life at home.

The years slipped away very slowly. My father had a very independent way of life, and made a comfortable living as a rabbit trapper during winter, a shepherd during spring lambing seasons, then clipping sheep and other work before returning to rabbit trapping when young rabbits were big enough to weigh 5 lb per couple.

Dad had a few very lovely ponies all of which had been broken to wear harness and pull a super large wheeled trap. Mother would often yoke the pony, and go out to wherever Dad was working, collect the coupled rabbits and drive them to the station at Mindrum, pack the couples into basketwork hampers and send them by train to mostly Leeds daily.

Dad would rent the rabbit catching from a few chosen farmers, paying up to £200 for the exclusive right to clear the rabbit population over the winter period, firstly by snares, and later when the winter set in by ferreting, catching the rabbits as they bolted out of the burrows, in nets, and with his rabbit dog or a double barrel shotgun.

We never seemed to want for anything, as we also kept a cow to milk, a couple of pigs to feed, a few hens, so we were always supplied with milk, butter, cream, salted sides of rolled bacon, hams, and rolled shoulders hanging from the ceiling, eggs by the dozen, a few rabbits each week. Our larder ofttimes was envied by the less well off, who could get round Mother for a bacon joint, a rabbit or whatever. We always had a happy home with an open door, and always someone in, to sing, play the piano or the fiddle, after the Border closed on a Saturday night at 10 p.m. Our round table, with a paraffin lamp in the middle, was a treat to so many of Dad's friends, who would be invited to tell stories or join in the music making. Mother was a very industrious baker, and her produce was quickly devoured.

Mother used to say "If there's fun to be had, your Dad will be there." So he was, with the happy knack of getting whoever was in his company to see the funny side of life. Later on in his 70s he had a birthday every month, with others through the week.

I remember him returning from a month's lambing and telling us he was going to start a pork butcher's business, in partnership with one Adam Goodfellow, so away went the pony and trap, and his year–old BSA motor bike, and the stable and cartshed got pulled apart [by] Cobham Builders, Morebattle, with tons and tons of cement converted the premises to a slaughterhouse, shop, and machine shop, and when nearly ready Adam Goodfellow flitted in to the Gypsy Palace. A Morris Cowley van appeared and they were ready to go. And go they did, after they had bought four pigs at St Boswells mart, which were transported to Kirk Yetholm by R & W Young, who by that time had a livestock lorry plying weekly to the livestock sales round the countryside.

The produce, in the way of pork, cooked meats, sausage, and all that pork butchers sold, went out in this van, each day of the week, driven alternatively by Adam and Dad. They became very successful, until two or three years later Adam decided he would go into business on his own in Coldstream. This changed Dad's ideas of partnership drastically, having gone to the expense of converting the premises, and providing the van. He then had to pay half of the business to Adam, who then had what was needed to start on his own.

We then had to employ a young pork butcher to help Dad on the road, which he did for about six or seven years, until Jimmy Blythe could take over.

Jimmy applied himself with great energy and soon became adept at producing and processing the cooked meats, and soon took over the job of slaughterman. The only thing he used to waste was the squeal, was his favourite description of what pork butchering was all about.

As I grew older I used to get more and more involved in all aspects of the business, which left little time to keep up with my school mates.

Jimmy was off work for a few days, which left Dad with some very long hours, to get the load ready for his van round. I remember meeting the van one day at the bottom of Dow Brae, as I went back to school after lunch. The van pulled up and Dad said "You'll have to come and help me slaughter a pig."

"But I've to get back to school now, I'll be home at 3.45 p.m."

"That's nae good you'll need to come now."

I was never back at school. How my father got round that I'll never know but at nearly 15 years of age I didn't care.

I then started work in the business, and slowly took over the work in the slaughterhouse, and the production of sausage making along with other prepared foods. This was before electricity was available, so the motive power for sausage mixer and mincer was a water–cooled petrol/paraffin internal combustion engine, coupled to the machine with a long belt.

The hot water system was even more basic in the form of a large boiler with a large lid, and a coal fire underneath. Cold water was one tap, which kept two half wooden barrels always brim full. The boiler was filled by bucket dipped into the barrels. The 'pot', as the boiler was called, had to have an ample supply of boiling water before we could start to de–hair the carcase of a pig in a large wooden tub some 8 ft. long, 3 ft. wide. and 3 ft deep, which required six large pails of bubbling boiling water mixed with two pails of cold, into which the pig was tipped. This correct temperature quickly loosened the hair, which was scraped off with a specially shaped scraper, and a sharp knife. Next the carcase was hoisted up by pulley, suspended from the rafters, the rope threaded over three pulley wheels at the top, and two on the bottom block allowed any of us to remove a 10 to 16 stone carcase from the hot water tub with very little effort. The intestines were then removed, and the carcase allowed to cool before further cutting up took place.

The remainder of the boiling water was slowly taken from the boiler a pailful at a time, mixed with a handul of washing soda, and the whole place scrubbed clean, and slushed off with pailfuls of cold water. The wooden benches and large wooden tables dried nearly white, as did the floors.

The van rounds were different daily. Tues and Sat as a 10 year old I used to accompany Dad, and would be sent to some of the doors, to knock or ring the bell and shout "Pork Butcher!" or politely invite the good lady to come and have a look in the van.

Jedburgh on Thursdays required a large load in the van of cooked meats cut and was most popular with the Rayon Mill workers. The "Artificial Silk" mill, as it was better known, stood in an area where the Bus Station and car park are now. There was a very large number of workers employed and many houses built to house them. Pork and its by–products were most popular, and my knock on a door was eagerly answered, and another customer would appear with a plate in one hand and purse in the other. I've seen it well past 8 p.m. before we got back on Thursday nights. The van then had to be scrubbed out and all the utensils washed up, before we had a meal. Friday, another early start and off to Wooler, with all the farm places on the way. This was another very busy day and a late wash–up.

Saturday, round Town Yetholm before lunch, and off to Kelso in the afternoon. As a boy I got off duty on Saturday, afternoons and proceeded to Kelso Library with my violin case for more music lessons from Mr Stimpson, which I've never forgotten and still pick up the violin Dad bought for me from Kerr the watchmaker. A violin then unvarnished made by Broomfield of Running Burn, by Kelso. After I could play Bluebells of Scotland and a few more tunes, Broomfield asked for the violin back so that he could varnish it. This job was half completed when Mrs Broomfield died, and very much later it was again back to Kerr's shop with an apology for botching the job of varnishing. As luck would have it, it sounded better than ever and still is a very valuable classic instrument.

This way of life became harder, after Dad returned one Monday with NO PIGS, as none were being offered for sale, but a few were obtained from farm workers round the area. This state of affairs lasted for a week or two, as apparently the price of fat pigs had not suited the normal suppliers, who stopped feeding pigs until sensible prices could again be had from the auction marts. The supplies having nearly dried up, saw prices for live pigs climb to wonderful prices for the seller, but quite useless for the pork butcher, so the shutters went up and, our livelihood gone, we had to think again.

Dad again surprised us all, when he told us that he had taken a herding at Halterburnhead, and would take over at the May term. What an upturn, we had to pack up and leave the home we children had had all our lives. However, Halterburnhead it was, with sound employment for Dad, only, luckily I quickly got a job as a butcher and worked at Wooler until the Army recruited myself and thousands more when War was declared in 1939. But that is another story for another time.

In the late 1920s and early 1930s a small cottage at one end of the lower Green was the home of the Cairns family — Mrs Cairns, her son Wullie, and daughter Jean. Jean had a peculiar way and always appeared to be chewing her words as she spoke to anyone.

My grandmother, next door to my parents, ran a small sweet and tobacconist's business, this was only six houses along from where Jean lived. The highlight of Jean's week was when she was sent to Grannie's shop for the weekly messages including "Sweeties for my Mother's MOOTH": Grannie was so amused at this request that she came over to Mother and told her what Jean had asked for, but wondered where else Mrs Cairns would put the sweets.

Next door to the small cottage was, and still is, a two–storey house which another of Mrs Cairns' daughters ran as a boarding house, and always had two of the local school teachers live in, and anyone else that required B & B. It was an immaculate house, and famous for the good food served.

The Old School and Dam, 1931–2

For many years my parents rented a byre next to the old school, where they kept a cow. Winter hay was stored in a tidy round stack in the adjacent stack yard. When I was 12 years old, Bob Waldie gave me a brood hen and 13 eggs, which I put to work in a home made coop, where the motherly clucking old hen sat for three weeks before surprising us all with 13 fluffy chicks following her round the stack yard. This was my introduction to 'poultry keeping'. I very quickly built up the numbers to 60, which were very profitable, with me delivering eggs all round the village at one shilling a dozen.

The Dam was always so lovely in those days, I soon had a dozen ducks, who enjoyed its clear water far more than I did. There was also a majestic drake, much larger than the ducks. When I set them loose from their night time accommodation one morning, the drake was missing. Poor old Duke, we suspected a fox had devoured him, and accepted that he was truly lost, as indeed he was, but later that week we learned of his whereabouts from an unusual source.

I was sent for by Agnes Young, who ran the village shop, where you could get anything from nails to needles, paraffin oil to oil lamps, and all the latest gossip and news. Agnes was a real artist when it came to extracting all the news from whoever went in, no matter what their age was. The story of the lovely Duke came out as follows: Mary, a 5 year old girl who lived with the Douglases across the road, told Agnes she had had a 'guid denner'. Agnes quickly learned the whole menu. Soup, tatties, cabbage and WHITE CRAW. This being new to Agnes, she said "Oh, Mary, that would be guid, but where did you get the white craw?"

"A dinna ken, Agnes, Canny catched it."

Canny, then in her mid 50s, could be seen daily with a great bundle of twigs and branches in a large hessian sheet, which she herself knew was far too heavy for her, but she got home with some queer kindling, as she could take a notion to anything she saw and could tuck it out of sight quick enough, like any true gypsy.

Jimmy Sharp and the Stones

The house on the right as you go down the hill to Allan Cottage was where Jimmy Sharp lived with his sister. Jimmy worked for the County Council Road Department and was engaged as long as I could remember breaking up great heaps of rock into bits the approx. size of an egg. The rocks were hewn in a small quarry at the Venchen and delivered to Jimmy, who used to make a big fuss as to where they were to be dumped from the steam–powered Foden tractor.

A large pile was dumped on the verge opposite the hut on the playing field. Jimmy with his light hammer on a long shank was about to start breaking up the chunks when a real worthy, Bobby Laidlaw, said "Man, Jimmy, if you take some of them over to the Bowmont and let them steep all night, they'll just crumble up when you hit them."

Jimmy, being everyone's stooge and very naive, was seen with a few large pieces in his arms, plodding to the Bowmont that night when he finished at 5 o'clock. Next day the rocks were as hard as ever, and angrily he told Bobby so when Bobby passed him, but Bobby told him "Jimmy, you have to lay them in, bed them down, for the water to soften them."

Jimmy had another try that night, with the same result in the morning, to be told by Bobby that they had brought him the "wrang kind o' stane", with which Jimmy agreed.
Naive Jimmy was, but he had a unique gift. Jimmy could whistle in tune louder than I've ever heard since. Kirk Yetholm knew when he shut his door and took off for work. As soon as his feet hit the ground, the piercing notes of Annie Laurie could be heard as he marched on, and even when he reached the Bowmont Bridge we could still recognise his choice for that morning. He could listen to a tune new to him, and immediately repeat it as sweetly as James Galway on his silver flute.

Johnnie Scott

Johnnie was a real character, who when I was a child from about 5 years of age was brought in to our house by my father, who really did enjoy his company and humour. He was a casual worker and had many skills.

Later, when I was 14, he had started a cycle retail business, part–time to start, but his ability as a bike builder soon spread, which kept him full–time. I bought a Raleigh racing bike from him for 25/–

The highlight of Johnnie's life was when Peggy Douglas accepted his proposal, and they were duly married in the Kirk. Messengers were sent to the Border Hotel to get him to the church on time.

The fun started when they came out. Honeymoons were not in fashion then, and he took Peggy home to her own house as Mrs Scott, and left for the Border, to drink her health while she made his tea.

Many of his friends were getting fou and unco happy by this time, but were delighted to see him again and offered congratulations to Mr Scott, who looked and reminded them he had just got married and he was Mr Douglas now.

The young men decided they would make preparations for the couple going home to Johnnie's own house, and with great care powdered the pillows with white flour, tied a loud ticking clock under the bed, and tipped a tin of Andrews Liver Salts into the chamber pot, and later about 10 p.m. escorted the newlyweds up "Muggers' Raw" to the door of the house. With best wishes and a few thumps on the back they left, but only to go round the corner, then get close to the window to hear Johnnie shouting to Peggy, who was more than a little deaf.

The mind boggles, but I'll leave it to your imagination to picture the scene. The pillows white, the heavy ticking under the bed, and Johnnie full of beer, and no toilet, except the Andrews Liver Salts-laced chamber pot. Johnnie unloaded a lot of his digested beer on top of the effervescing Andrews Liver Salts, and with bubbles foaming over the top he could not lay it down. Peggy, shocked at the sight, said in a shrill voice "What's wrang wi' ye, Johnnie, ye're fizzing." It put the fear of death in Johnnie, who very tenderly said "Oh Peggy did you see a ghost, you're as white as sna', and your heart is fair thumping, I can hear it from ower here."

We had to leave them to it after that, or they would surely have found us, had we lingered any longer.

Auld Yetholm in the 1930s and 1940s

by Doug Turnbull

In my lifetime the village has changed out of all character. It is no longer the close knit community of families we were brought up with and cherished. Today we have a new community of complete strangers who have bought properties and moved in, taking over most of the social activities.

Let's go back to the old days. At the bottom of the east end of the village below the Kelso turn–off lived John Christie, a good joiner with two daughters, Eleanor and Betty. I went to school with Betty in the 30s. Next door in the Old Manse Mrs Trevelyan resided. A bit of an eccentric, she kept a Riley car with a two–seat 'dickie', open to all weathers. I had some happy times looking after that car; driving it was joy when you were only 17. Over the road, the school next comes to mind with Mr Jenkins, Headmaster, and female teachers – a Miss Jamieson, Miss Roberston and Miss Gilmour. The school had quite a large catchment area. Farm workers' children walked in from Shotton, the Moffats from Old Graden, the Patersons and Dodds from Lochside, Wat Nichol from Woodside, and others from all farms in between – a good walk in all weathers with a flask or a tin bottle of tea and some doorstep 'jammy piece'. There was no cycling then and no school bus. In the winter Bell Hay had a soup kitchen which provided a hot meal on some cold winter days. Good tackity boots were the norm for the long daily walks.

The garage came next and Jocky Stenhouse for petrol, repairs and taxis – a life I was to become very familiar with. Jocky employed a few people, Willie Watson and other drivers. He had two petrol pumps and sometimes sold it at a pennyworth in a bottle! As an agent for cycles "Perry" comes to mind but such were beyond the reach financially of nearly all of us at school. We made do with old boneshakers usually acquired from John Scott (The Rat) at Kirk Yetholm for a "couple of bob". He had an outhouse behind the Border Hotel where he made up bikes of all descriptions.

Moving up the village past Whitelaw's byre and field, where he kept hens and cows, we come to Bell Hay, who lived in the bottom house which faced the Kelso road end. She cleaned the school and made the soup in the winter. Next, Davy Colville and his wife – a man getting on in years, who was an evangelist. He built the mission hall which still stands today and where meetings were held and various preachers came. "Jumbo Smith" was another such local preacher. He held outdoor meetings where a small portable organ was carried out with a lantern for light. Tibbie Herbert used to play the organ for him.

Andrew Johnson lived down there. He was a man of means as I remember. Then came Maggie "Gled" – Gladstone – and her son Eric. Thereafter was a spare bit of land where the ex–police houses stand today. Then came the smiddy yard of ``Wullie Gled". The blacksmith's was a busy place, shoeing horses and doing other chores relevant to the farrier. It was also a meeting place for local men who were out of work. Archie Gladstone and his wife, Bunt, lived above Wullie and his family in the adjoining house. Archie drove the baker's van for Tice. Two men went on the baker's van. This was a legacy from the horse drawn era when Wullie Stenhouse was vanman. He never did learn to drive so "Wullie the bread" as he was known sold the wares and Archie Gled drove the van.

Across the Dow Brae road was Jocky "Fistie". He had only one hand and herded the cows. Next door were the Tokely family – four boys and two girls. Martin was my best pal for adolescent years but sadly he died in Ireland and not an old man. He was a hunt servant and learned his craft with the College Valley hunt. Then we come to Johnnie Davidson – "Splash" and Jeanie (who was an Adams) with two girls. Andrew Chapman was next, round the corner facing the Green. He drove for R. Young's haulage. Jocky Wilson lived alone and worked at Old Graden with the famous Eck Rae. Then next door was auld Ritchie Stenhouse, uncle Wull and Bessie, and cousins Mae and Alice.

Next came the baker shop with Maggie Kennedy, who was Tice the baker's wife. They employed bakers. Ritchie Tice and Wullie Kennedy all turned out bread, tea bread, pies, cakes for a fair catchment area. I can remember a loaf of bread costing 2p and a pie 2p in the 1930s. Next along we had Dixon Turnbull and Maggie. They had a grocer's shop at one time but the advent of the supermarkets killed off most of these small shops. Their daughter Elma was a school teacher who married Yair Goodfellow who, sadly, died a young man. They had a son, also Yair, who now lives in Edinburgh.

Jocky Wakeford, or "Rinkie" as he was known, came next in his Border Boot Store. He had a nice little business doing repairs to all types of footwear, and also sold new boots and shoes. During the war he advertised with little cards in his shop window. One comes to mind: "Aeroplane quality, sub–marine prices." Another was "Gang North, gang South, gang East, gang West, strong boots will make your pander." "There's Rogersons in the North and Wakefords in the Borders." So you see the power of advertising even then!

Coming next were Jimmy Nichol and Isa; then John Weir, who was a retired farmer and well–to–do. He used to castrate the lambs at Duncanhaugh Mill and pulled the testicles with his teeth. As boys we helped to catch the lambs. I remember his face smeared with blood, and now and again the smell of meths. It must have been used as a disinfectant. Next door we had a good grocer's shop. Armstrong was the first owner I can remember. He got a consignment of toilet rolls, the first in Yetholm, and on telling Stovie Jock the purpose of these, he said "I'll not be needing them – a cut a' mine's clean." This business was taken over and built up by William Hardie before and during the war. Sibbald's came in 1948–49 as the Hardie's only son, Jim, was not interested in carrying on. He bought a garage business in Melrose and sold Austin cars. Jim died a youngish man and his mother, Mrs Hardie, retired to Denholm.

Further along was Wait's shop – sweets and papers. Maid looked after the shop and we could buy a halfpennyworth of mixed sweets. A pennyworth was a big bagful. How they ever made a profit I'll never know! Daily papers were delivered to Kirk Yetholm by various school–leavers. Our first fags were bought there: 5 Woodbines for two pence and up the Haugh for a smoke. Sometimes we were sick as dogs and got a beating when we got home stinking of baccy. Happy days! All of us kids loved Maid Wait. She was a good and generous person. Eventually I sorted the Sunday papers for her during the war and as sweets were rationed then, I always got paid in kind, which was great then.

The Temperance Hotel adjoining, with Dave and Nell Riddell, was a boarding house–cum–hotel. They were elderly when I was a boy. Dave was a character. An expression of his was "Ya hoondy brut." I always remember that they kept a cow in the back outhouse which was grazed on the haugh common land.

The Plough Hotel, which still flourishes today, has in my time had many tenants. As they say, we have seen them come and go. A wee Glasgow man, Jim Bowie, took over after the war and I think did rather well. Of course he was in at a good time as this was the only place to go: no telly then or other distractions. We rarely had pushbikes to travel with. Jean Turnbull lived next door – "Chipper Jean" as she was known because she had once run a wee chip shop. Lizabeth Cairns, or "Squeaky" as we named her, lived on her own and was very much into religion. She was a nice wee soul. Then, as now, came the butcher's shop of Geordie Lees, the master. Tom Allan served his time with him and was there until he retired. A George Cairns had previously had a tailor's shop there and had lived above the premises. He was followed by the Smiths and then the Underwoods. Mrs Underwood was a war widow, her husband being lost at sea in the Merchant Navy. Her family comprised Sheila, John and George, known as 'Poddie'.

Round the corner was the Club – as long as I can remember with billiard tables and various pastimes. It was a good going concern until the 60s when it went into decline. The building is still in process of being repaired. When I was a youth the butcher's corner had a crowd of older men congregated there on Sunday nights. The "crack" was always great, and as a boy I loved to stand and listen – all part of my education. Pubs and clubs were closed: the Sabbath day of course! The world was put to rights. Many of these men were either casual workers, rabbit catchers or farmhands – all poor and honest men. The war came and created a lot more employment, better wages and conditions. Many were also called up to the Forces, as was my own father. I vividly remember him going to Carlisle and how we looked through a map to find it. My father was a DEMS anti–aircraft gunner and was on merchant ships until he was based in Malta, where he remained all through the siege years. Sadly he died just a few years after the war ended.

Now we come to the back road – now Grafton Road. The four new Council houses housed Ritchie Tice the baker; the Cockburns – Dan and Bell, Wullie, Jimmy and Buttie. Then our family – Mother, me, Peter and Hamish. Then the end house which was occupied by Jim Whitelaw and his wife and one daughter, Margaret, who ended up in Australia. Below them was the mission hall, which still stands today. In front of it stood the thatched house in which the Allans lived. John Allan was a postman and also a saddler and a very clever engineer. Jock, May and Tommy Allan were good playmates pre–war. Jock was older than me and a very clever chap with his hands. If Jock had been educated and trained he would have gone places – a good mind wasted! On the corner we come to Grafton House and Danny and Mary Oliver. Opposite were Bob Herbert and Tibbie his daughter. Bob was a very good mason, and Tibbie herself went on to be a leading light in the community over many years as village registrar, librarian, Shepherds' Show secretary and village representative on many committees and also as a councillor. She was awarded the M.B.E. later in her life. Ale Fox lived alone next door in a biggish house. The Fox family had been blacksmiths and Ale was the last surviving daughter. She never married. She was known as "Foosham". I remember she had two evacuees during the war and the older one, George Summers, I knew at school. He too got the nick-name, "Foosham".

Further on John and Maggie Cairns were next. John, a roadman, was originally from the family which had owned the land and had run Blunty's Mill making blankets. This mill was water powered and was fed from a dam at Hayhope. The water drove a sawmill and a corn mill before reaching Blunty's. Next door were the Butlers, a roof slater and family. The Butlers had three sons, Will, John and Robin. Their daughter, Alison, became my wife. The oldest son, Will, was killed on a bombing raid over Germany during the war. After them came Wullie Turnbull, wife Mary and daughter Wilma. He drove the Hardies' van first, and later Wood the baker's. He eventually took a pub in Spittal at Tweedmouth.

Down the "Wee Roadie" are two bungalows built pre–war for £400, which I suppose was a lot of money then. Money is nothing until you have none, so they say! The Robertsons, Lucy and her mother, of the bootmakers in Kelso, lived in the first. Then came the bungalow of Ritchie Stenhouse, his wife Lucy and daughter Shona, who now lives in Gordon. Craig, the builder from Acriston, built a wooden house which still stands, near the bottom. Across the road is another bungalow which was owned by Elizabeth Laidlaw who lived there. All the additional bungalows seen today were built after the war. Near to them in Yewtree Road is a large yew which is reputed by experts to have been planted after the Battle of Flodden. It was the custom then to plant a yew tree after a national disaster.

Back to the main road and on the left to the thriving market gardening business of Tam Nichol, who was a joiner by trade. In the 30s he had lots of glass for tomatoes – a real luxury then – and he also specialised in "Kelsae Onion" plants. The son Robert ended up as gardener and handyman at Romany House old folk's home, as it became.

The house next along, now called Bowmont Lodge, was the home of Mr Mather, the headmaster, and later Miss Cowan Douglas, a good artist. She built the studio extension which is still there today.

The Manse comes next, standing in a wooded garden. The minister was the Rev.Robert Macalister and his church was that of the Wee Frees at the top of Dow Brae, where the Gibsons now have a caravan park. I can remember as an apprentice with Frank Gibson when he bought the kirk and the field.

The Wauchope Hall was also once a kirk but I cannot remember it as such. So we were well off for kirks at one time and the spiritual needs of Yetholm were well catered for. There were also two missions, one at the tin hut built by David Colville, and one in a single room at Bywell which was Jumbo Smith's – Jumbo because he was a large ex–seafaring man with a booming voice. He also went out to the Swan Hotel corner with a little portable organ and sang and preached. One song comes to mind. It was "Throw out the lifeline, someone is drifting away", sung to a good tune. I don't think he had many converts.

Beyond the Free Church manse stood Romany House, built by Dr Rodger, a local G.P. He must have had a few bob! I recall Bobby Douglas ("Croxie") telling me that he carted stones to build it from a quarry on Hayhope Hill. Later owners, the Muirheads, had it as an upmarket hotel. They had two daughters, Jeany and Ramsay, and a younger son Gilbert, with whom I went to Kelso High School during the war. He later became a dentist and practised in Galashiels. The semis across from Romany were built in the 1930s by a Branxton firm for £500 a throw, which was then a lot of money. Occupants at that time were a Mrs Elliot, the Dingwalls and a retired Dr Davidson. Next down the road was Geordie Simpson's stackyard and sheds, where today the new Council houses stand, and then the track up the brae.

Heading down back to the village and facing the market garden we come first to Grannie Cowan's, and next to Garnet Tice, then to Jumbo Smith followed by Tam Nichol's. In the thatched cottage next door lived a family evacuated from Edinburgh during the war and whose name escapes me. In Hirsel Cottage were the Olivers, Violet being the lady of the house. Dave Montgomery came next. He was estate manager for Wauchope and responsible for maintenance, etc. Jack Stenhouse and Carrick Wood were his assistant estate workers.

Dave's building was later occupied by Vera and Peter Darling. Vera was the only daughter and she and Peter lived there for many years. They sold it when Peter retired and moved into an old folk's flat. Dan Robson and Reena his daughter were the next down. He had been in the White Swan for many years and was married to my great–aunt Bella, who was a Turnbull. Her parents (my great–grandparents) were previously in the White Swan.

In the next detached cottage lived David Cotton[1], a widower, and his daughter Ann. He had a lot of gardens in which he grew a large quantity of fruit. As boys we used to pick blackcurrants and raspberries for a penny a pound. The weigh–in was always a disappointment as we always thought we had more than the scaled weight. But it was a good source of sweetie money, even though we were rationed to four ounces a week during the war, and had to tender a coupon from the ration book.

We were always well fed in wartime, Mother being a marvellous cook, and as my gran Turnbull kept hens and bantams, we never went short of eggs. The Pavelys lived in "Hilton View" – Mrs Pavely, old Grannie Quinn and four of a family. Bill and Margaret being the older, I went to the High School in Kelso with them. The two younger boys did rather well, both training as doctors of medicine after National Service.

Across the opening was Rose Cottage, where lived my grandparents and two aunts – Jen and Jean. My Grannie was a tremendous character, and a good crack always. If ever my brothers or I needed anything, that was where we went. Money? A penny, for what it would buy, was a great treat. When I did my National Service and came home on leave or was going back, she would give me a ten–shilling note, produced from a pail filled with bran mash, which she used for the hens she kept in a field down towards the Haugh. This was a secret cache from my aunts. Then back in the house she would tell the two of them to "Get the laddie something!" So I scored again with two half–crowns. That was a lot of money in 1948. Happy memories!

Up the wee vennel at Montgomery Place lived Dave Hay, his wife Meg and Dod, who was a school pal. Dave drove a bus for Jock Stenhouse (the Pinter) who ran the local garage next to the school. One of the runs Dave did was to Otterburn via Jedburgh. So they were quite ambitious in those days, Dod and I on odd occasions got a free hurl. Next in Montgomery Place was Mr Sutherland and his daughter Katie. I think that he was a postman. Then came the Old Brewery which was used by Hardie the grocer as a garage,

---

[1] David Cotton was the son of an Edinburgh lawyer and brought up and educated in comparative luxury. He trained as a mining engineer and spent most of his working life in North America. He retired finally to Yetholm and filled his time creating a market garden across the road from his detached cottage. He experimentally grew potatoes planted in the autumn alongside those planted conventionally in the spring, and found the earlier planting gave a better return. Autumn planting is now being advocated as a way of spreadng the workload from the overloaded spring. So David Cotton was ahead of his time! He was unconventional in many ways. He was a convinced pro–Soviet communist and held strongly atheistic views and was vehemently intolerant of the Kirk and all it stood for.

with meal and grain store above. This once had been used as our Scout hall, I being in the Cubs 1936–38. Willie Turnbull the slater and family lived next door. My wife's father, Robert Butler, came to work with him before starting up on his own. Next were the Watsons. Toby was a cobbler. Willie and Bert were his sons. Willie was a mechanic and Bert a baker. The Simpsons were their neighbours in what had once been a butcher's shop. George, the son, had a smallholding in the village. There were quite a few small–time farmers in the village at that time. Most of the fields around the village were divided up between them – and they all made a living. George Simpson married Lizzie Armstrong, daughter of the grocer, who was in the shop before Hardie – the quality grocer. Across the gap we get to the White Swan Hotel – the most popular pub in the village. Jack and Kit Johnson made perfect mine hosts. Jack hailed from Longtown and had trained as an architect – an educated man. Kitty was from the Western Isles and a very good–hearted person. Jack was a pigeon fancier and kept and supplied pigeons as carriers during the war.

Turning directly up the Green we come to the house of Allan the saddler. The post office next door further down the Green was kept by Mrs Walker with two girls, Annie and Margaret. Her husband, a ship's captain, had been lost at sea during the war. Next door the Adams family had started a shop selling sweeties, fags and papers. Old John and his son Alec attended the shop. They had a nice wee business but there was plenty of competition. Today they have a monopoly which can be a bad thing. At one time Maid Wait delivered papers, but today it is, come for a paper or do without! How grand it would be if they started to deliver again. For a small fee I'm sure a schoolboy would welcome such a job. Chat Lillie and Pheamie were next door. He had been a game dealer and behind the house, up the Dodds opening, he had stables and premises on the back road. The Dodds family, with Geordie, Jim and their sisters, had a farm steading where the new houses at Deanfield now stand. Their house, which is next to the Green, could be the oldest house in Yetholm: Jim claims so. Jim and his wife still live in the house. The stackyard was also there and I can remember the thresher coming in, pulled by a steam traction engine and the hustle and activity at the threshings. Labour was provided through the local farmers' ring as previously mentioned. One helped the other and this was reciprocated.

The Gowenlocks were next down – George and his sister Jenny. They had previously farmed at Duncanhaugh Mill with their brother John. They were an old Yetholm family and had a married sister in Mrs Hogg, whose husband was a school teacher. They had a son who was a doctor of medicine. Next again was Johnny Hogg, who was another smallholder. Lizzie Bolton lived with him and looked after him. Known as "Punton" Hogg, I can just recall him. Next down were Jimmy and Tibby Young with two of a family – Rosemary and George. Jimmy had some fields, outhouses and sheds at the end of Deanfield Road. He was a general dealer and kept sheep, cows and hens. I worked for Jimmy when I was at school during the war. One task I had was to feed the sheep which were up the loaning, which meant carrying up a bag of oats to fill the feed boxes. I had then to count them, wait until they were fed and then to turn the boxes over to keep them free of rain. I didn't bother after a while and just left them feeding. When Jimmy found out there was hell to pay! Getting sixpence a week for this, I was the envy of some of my school pals.

Yes, times were hard then, but we were happy. What you've never had you'll never miss! Food and sweets were rationed but we were well enough fed. We got cod liver oil and Horlicks tablets at school, and with plenty of rabbits and the odd pheasant and hare, nobody went hungry.

The grocer's shop run by John Christie and his wife was next down. Of their two boys, Jackie and Francis, Francis was to take over the business. John Christie was called up for service in the wartime army and Mrs Christie to her credit carried on with a Mary Murray, who came to help out. I too got a job there at weekends. I went round Kirk Yetholm customers on a Friday night, took their orders and delivered them by basket on a cycle on Saturday. Next door to the shop, where Gibson's garage now stands, was a thatched house fronted by a garden on half a side. A family Gillies lived there followed by Gibsons and then an old lady, Mrs Goodfellow, who lived in a part of it. During Halloween the old lady had us, the guisers, call every night of the week. We sometimes got a sweetie or a jeely piece for our efforts, but never any money! The poor old soul would be living on a pittance.There was no TV then and hardly a radio. The sets required both a dry and a wet battery, the latter being re–charged about once a week at the garage for sixpence. Jimmy Quinn was an apprentice after me and his job was battery charging in a little shed. He charged and replaced them daily. David Cotton came back one day and complained to Jimmy that his battery was not charged. He had got only two tunes from it. To which Jimmy replied, "No bad, threepence a tune!" He got a severe telling off for that.

Mr and Mrs Wagstaffe lived in the next house. He was known as "Auld Waggie". He had spent some time in America. Waggy had a good lurcher dog called Sam, which kept his pot boiling for many years: in those days most families kept a good poaching dog. It had to be able to hunt and to kill and to carry, and was preferably soft mouthed. Ideally a rabbit would be brought to hand still living and unbruised. Beyond his place was the Wauchope Hall, where we played badminton or held and ran dances on Friday nights until 1.30 a.m. Saturday night hops ended at 11.30 p.m. as the Sabbath loomed and we had to be out by then. The bands varied so much. Usually they were accordions and fiddles. One of the best was that of Monty Strachan. Jack Proud of Coldstream also had an excellent band.

Below the Wauchope Hall you came to a house and shop belonging to Mr Somerville, a grocer, but which was taken over by George Cairns, a tailor and draper. He made me my first sports coat. You could not buy suits off the peg then as you can nowadays. I remember a pal buying a pocket watch from George Cairns and was showing it off to old Tice the baker. Tice made the comment that if it broke or stopped, George Cairns the tailor couldn't sort it. Sound advice then!

Down from the shop towards the main road you came first to a Mrs Elander, then Mr G. Simpson and then Jocky Stenhouse, the garage proprietor who moved in when he left the bungalow at the garage. Willie Watson was next door with his wife Peggy and son John. Willie worked at the garage before he went to work in Kelso at Turnbull's sawmill as an engineer maintaining transport. Willie cycled back and forth every day for years, in all weathers. I myself cycled to Kelso daily for one year when I left the High School to work at Henderson's. I often accompanied Willie on the journey home. This was during the war. It was a great day for me when Frank Gibson and his then partner, Hogg Fairbairn, bought the garage and took me on as their first apprentice. No more having to tackle that road!

Tom and Johnnie Hogg lived at the end of the row next to the road. Jeannie Martin, their niece, looked after them, and Tom Martin, a nephew, worked for them. They had a small farm, the stables being at the back of the premises. Jeannie had a milk round in the village, all delivered in pitchers by the Tokely family. You could buy a pennyworth of skimmed milk, which would make a good rice pudding, in those times. We boys were never far away from the Hoggs.

During school holidays I was always friendly with the Tokely boys and as they were Jeannie's nephews we got the inside turn. I was specially friendly with Martin Tokely. Martin used to ride their high–stepping pony. When this animal got a switch with a whip it could fly. What a beast! It did not gallop, but trotted, lifting its front hooves very high. Old Tom Hogg used to break in his own workhorses, Clydesdales, which he also bred. He kept the mares only because in those days stallions were travelled round the districts to be mated with the mares.

I see I have missed out a street so will start from the old Post Office on the Green and head back south–west towards the Nursery Wood from Allan the saddler's. Next to him was a Mary Messer, who kept a little barking terrier, next door the Grays, Jim and Maim with two sons John and Derek. John was very clever and got educated. He became a minister and ended up as a professor of languages, that being his field. Derek served his time with Dalgleish and became a baker. He served in the navy, was a wartime prisoner of the Japanese and had a rough time in Burma. Derek married a local girl, Maime Winton, who was the gardener's daughter from Cherrytrees. Derek lived and worked in Gala until his death a few years ago. Captain Webster and his housekeeper were next along. He was an old man and seldom seen in the village. Beyond him at Balcherry lived a Newcastle woman but I cannot recall her name. Beyond her was a Mr Newlands.

Then came the police station and P.C. Bert Smith, his wife and daughter Margaret, who was in my class at school. Margaret herself later joined the police force in Edinburgh. Further on across the road in a house that no longer exists – a thatched house – lived Dod Young, a postman and his wife. They had two daughters, Joan and Jean, and a son, John – all older than me. I remember John being hit in the eye by a flying object at school. He was very fortunate not to lose the eye. He became a teacher and later an accountant. When Dod retired he ordered a new Ford Anglia and built a wooden garage for it, which I now own. Dod was in hospital when the new car arrived so John, his son, took it down to let him see it. Dod viewed it from the hospital ward and saw mainly the roof. Sadly that was all he saw of his new Ford before he died.

The next thatched house was known to us as Grannie Cowan's, she being the occupant. Then we had the Woods family – Joey, Maggie, Carrick, Jock and Wilma. I can remember Joey as the hall caretaker and Carrick working on the Wauchope estate doing fencing, etc. He also worked at the sawmill on the Haugh, which was powered by water fed from the Bowmont. Jock was a baker and Wilma was on the buses as a conductress. Next along came the Laidlaws. I can just remember old Jane Laidlaw and some of her very large family – Hughie, Jimmy, Bobby, Johnnie, Wull, Eckie, Queenie, Katie and Muriel come to mind. Hughie was a baker and went into business at Morebattle. He played cricket for Yetholm and was a fast bowler. After the war he played for Morebattle. Bobby and Wull had various jobs – rabbit catchers being every winter's occupation. I remember Bobby as a great storyteller with a great sense of humour. He also liked a drink. His sister Muriel Laidlaw married Jim MacGregor who herded at Halterburn and later retired into the village.

Eck Laidlaw was the Young Men's Club caretaker. Every New Year's Day the cricket club ran a big domino match and Dixon Turnbull was the mainstay and organiser. It was a double entry and the matches were played both in the Wauchope Hall and at the club. If any of the Laidlaw brothers met in the first round it was known there would be ructions as it meant that one would be knocked out. Dixon must have been sorely tried on many occasions. These competitions were then supported by large numbers of men, all workers from surrounding farms and many Yetholm village supporters, The pubs did a roaring trade, as this was for many the holiday and highlight of the year. We as boys enjoyed all this but only as spectators. I have never seen so many drunk men since those days. They did enjoy themselves!

Willie Stenhouse and Jenny had one son, John. They were to become our neighbours in later years. John became an accountant and worked in Kelso until he retired. He married Mary Lauder and had a son, Billy. Sadly Billy died a young man. Willie himself was a great character. He killed rabbits, did lambings and clippings, mainly at Cherrytrees. Jenny had at one time been cook for the Marshalls at Cherrytrees and Willie had served his time as a baker in Yetholm with Ritchie Stenhouse, his uncle, in earlier years.

The last house along the row was the home of Jim Martin and his wife Mary. I remember the sons Jimmy and Tom, and daughters Annie, Nina and Ruth. Annie became mother of the Tokely family. Across the way were the outhouses and byre where the cows were milked daily. The main buildings which comprised their farm were at the Old Brewery. The stable was there and another byre, with other buildings housing cattle and pigs, and there was also storage for hay and fodder. Their acreage of fields was up the loaning towards Yetholm Law. They also ran another milk round in the village. Latterly it was Jimmy who became the mainstay and farmer. At that time he and his wife Lucy were living above the nearby ex–blacksmith's shop. They had one daughter, Muriel, who is now Mrs Harvey.

A Childhood in Kirk Yetholm

by Alastair Turnbull

The Kirk Yetholm of my youth has gone for ever. Sad in many ways, but most of the poverty has now gone, which must be good.

My father, the village doctor, came to Yetholm about 1936, some five years before I was born. Our home faced onto the Green. We always had staff – live–in maid, daily woman, nanny (who also lived in), gardener.

There was much sub–standard housing in Kirk Yetholm, many with outside toilets, but reform was on the way. Four prefabs arrived in the village, cream–coloured like those I saw in Edinburgh. One of our dailies lived in one – kitchen, sitting–room, bathroom, two bedrooms. My memories of it are that it was comfortable but it must have been very small and cold. Town Yetholm had grey prefabs with flat roofs. There was a tiny house, now demolished, in what is now the car park outside the kirk. A village home with which I was familiar was at the foot of Kirk Yetholm High Street, on the corner. There was a former smiddy downstairs, not in action in my time, but the family, named Young, all lived upstairs in two rooms and a tiny kitchen. Andrew Young, who was a rabbit catcher, kept ferrets and had a pony and cart.

Father held surgeries in our house at 11 am and 6.30 pm Patients waited in the hall. Medicines were ordered by phone at lunchtime and Father brought them up from Kelso in the late afternoon. Every prescription was wrapped in white paper, sealed with red wax and the patient's name and address were handwritten. Medicines were left in the porch and patients helped themselves! Father visited more patients than came to surgery: he had visiting rounds in the village, in Morebattle, outlying farms and the Bowmont and Kale valleys. His partner was Dr Davidson, who practised in Kelso, and Father would meet up with him every afternoon. He had Thursday afternoon and evening off, but otherwise was on call day and night.

With my sister and brother, I was fully integrated with village life, using such Kirk Yetholm words as deek, jugal, rage, cuffy, donart. Men gathered for a "crack" in Kirk Yetholm Main Street, in their flat caps and collarless shirts, talking, putting the world to rights. I jealously guard Scottish culture and fear the day when Scots will be no longer spoken in the school playground.

My first school was what our family called "Dodds' Academy". It was run by Miss Sarah Dodds, and it was attended by genteel little children, for whom the village school was considered too rough! Apart from "lessons" in the Dodds' house, we also had them at our house, The Green, and at Lochside. Admiral Oliver of Lochside was off fighting in the war, as were the tenants of Lochside.

The pupils of Dodds' Academy were allowed to go on the annual Spittal Trip, but much to our annoyance we were segregated from the primary school children and were herded by Miss Dodds to the rocks at the far end of Spittal beach!

And so to Yetholm Primary, where I was a pupil for two years. The teachers were Mrs Clark, who lived at Crookedshaws, and then Mrs Tice, sister–in–law of the baker. The headmaster was Mr Jenkins, who ended his days in New Zealand. I seem to remember writing on slates in Mrs Clark's class. We sat at tiered desks, and in Mrs Tice's class our marks were totted up weekly and we sat in order of merit, changing places every week. Billy Younger never moved from the top of the class. His family lived at Currburn.

Mrs Tice used to administer the tawse to backsliders. We had lunch in a building, now demolished, in the playground, cooked by a Mrs Davidson and I think Mrs Gladstone. We were made to drink Council supplied milk at elevenses. I remember hating this on frosty mornings, and can still smell it.

We must have been some of the first pupils in Yetholm to have radio lessons – on the Scottish Home Service – for which there were accompanying booklets. Boys and girls entered the school from different entrances. The outside toilets stank.

Having been born in 1941, my memories of the Second World War are fragmentary, but I definitely remember gas masks hanging next to our back door;

blackout screens tailored to the size of the windows; my Father's Home Guard uniform; trenches at the top of the Halterburn road where the Home Guard practised; and in the playing field Army huts which lasted for many years. Troops were billeted there after Dunkirk, their officers living in Yetholm Hall. There were several "D.P.s" (Displaced Persons) in the village: we had one as a gardener at The Green.

Mr Robson, who wore a navy blue uniform, was probably a "plane spotter" as a member of the Royal Observer Corps.

The weather was very hot in summer and very cold in winter. Fishing for trout in the Bowmont was a regular pastime. I would fish often and always came home with trout large enough to fry. There are no longer the same amount of fish in the river, largely due I think to farm chemicals. I can still point out the good places to fish.

In those days the Council did not cut the grass on the Green, and in the summer those villagers who kept ponies would cut circles and make hay. We children used to play endlessly in these circles while the grass grew high around us. In very hot weather a great treat was to borrow the Youngs' galvanised bath and fill it wth cold water in the garden at The Green.

I remember the big flood of 1947/1948, when the bridges at Yetholm Mains, Hayhope, Attonburn and the end of the Blakelaw straight were all swept away. They were replaced by Bailey bridges. Much disruption was caused for a long time. Lochtower had only the lower road into it, and it would regularly flood for weeks on end.

Winters were very cold, but we accepted this as we knew no better, and of course there was no central heating. Again, 1947–1948 saw major snow storms, and we built igloos on Kirk Yetholm Green. One year the Yetholm Mains road was blocked for well over a month; the cutting below the Border Hotel was totally full of snow, and the snow was still banked up at Easter.

At harvest time, corn was cut by binders and stooked, followed by a visit of the travelling threshing machine. The "feenishing" was an occasion: village boys would wait with their dogs until almost the end of the cut when the rabbits and hares would break cover.

In Kirk Yetholm, animals were everywhere. The village was alive with dogs – lurchers, greyhounds, sheepdogs, mongrels. They moved freely, with no restrictions on dog litter! Various families kept cows for milking. Will

Whitelaw had a tiny byre (now demolished) opposite the Youth Hostel. John Anderson kept geese on the Green (the geese were fascinated by my Father and would chase him). Most families kept hens. Horses were often grazed on the Green. Various residents had horses and cats. Rabbit catching was a major pastime, and many people kept ferrets. On the farms, most cottages had pigsties, and farm workers would keep a pig.

Kirk Yetholm got its water supply from Staerough. There was a collecting tank in the Fair Park field, which we could see from our house. There were several street pumps – at the end of Young's garage, up the Halterburn road, one in the middle of the Green and one opposite the Veitches' house. All were used. I particularly remember Jean Ferguson and 'Nanny' Douglas (Charlie Douglas' sister) filling their buckets. They wore sacks as aprons. The house of Belle Young (my nanny from earlier) was grander as it had a cold–water tap in the downstairs smiddy. Yetholm must have been connected to the electricity mains before the war, but I do remember paraffin lamps and generators in outlying farms. There were oil lamps on Kirk Yetholm Green, as there was one outside our house, which was lit by Charlie Douglas. These were replaced by weak electric lights on the existing poles.

Charlie Douglas also collected the village rubbish in his horse and cart. It was taken to a dump at the foot of the Venchen Hill, accessed from the Cherrytrees road. It was screened by green corrugated sheeting.

My first sight of television was at the Coronation, in 1953. John Anderson (the geese owner) was a butcher who worked in Kelso and lived in the house now occupied by the Sangsters. His was the first TV in Kirk Yetholm and he invited many from the village to watch the Coronation.

Other TV sets then appeared, but the nearest aerial was at Kirk o' Shotts, between Edinburgh and Glasgow. Big house aerials appeared in the village but the pictures were very poor. Morebattle had better reception.

Then the Jedforest TV Line Company arrived! In Kirk Yetholm they set up an aerial at the foot of Staerough and a line was fed to any subscribers who wanted the service in Town Yetholm and Kirk Yetholm. We received bills based on a weekly charge. I can't remember the date all this happened, but it was still in operation in 1967. Eventually a BBC aerial was raised near Hospital Wood and Yetholm received a satisfactory public TV service.

In 1950 I was prised away from Yetholm Primary School and sent to a prep school near Newbridge, Midlothian. Five years later found me at Sedbergh

School, in Yorkshire. It was a tough disciplinarian upbringing, but none the worse for that. Then from 1960–65 Edinburgh University, MA LLB, then working in Edinburgh, then coming back home in 1967.

Bob Wood had the baker shop in Kirk Yetholm (now the house with bow windows). The shop was on the right, and the bakehouse on the left. Mrs Wood, who served in the shop, called all women customers "Hen". The bakers were Bob Wood and Fid Veitch. The Woods had a travelling van, driven by Johnny McGeechie, who was from Glasgow. We had an account with Wood the baker, in respect of which there was a notebook headed on the front: "Mrs Dr Turnbull". I remember that the Woods' telephone in the back shop was a black upright of the "Daffodil" design, with an earpiece that one took off the hook, which alerted the operator in Town Yetholm exchange, who said "Number please".

Travelling vans played an important part in village life Kelso Co–op sent grocery vans and a "Fleshing" van, but they never stopped at our house. There were also clothes vans, sometimes driven by Indians, who also did door to door calls: as a boy I found them quite frightening!

One of the vans that visited regularly was a circulating library, run by a Mr Telfer, who I think came from Wooler. My father got his library books that way. My Mother was grander: her books were sent monthly from Edinburgh – Grant's in George Street. Yetholm had its own library, looked after at that time by Mr Wagstaffe. The village library later moved to the school and for years was run by Tibbie Herbert.

Milk was originally delivered in a horse and cart by a Mr Cartner, who had a dairy farm at Yetholm Mill. We would take a container to the cart and the milk was poured from a bucket! Later the milk came from Pawston: this was very upmarket as the milk came in sealed wax cartons with brown writing: "A.C. Straker, Pawston". Then John Milligan started producing milk at Yetholm Mill and delivered it himself.

Tice was the baker in Town Yetholm. He also had a delivery van, driven by Sheena Davidson Their shop, which was next to Adams' shop, doubled as telephone exchange and post office. I remember the exchange with its leads. Probably there were about 50 telephones in the village, originally with single or double digit numbers. There were at least three postmen, with bicycles. The postmen's beats were Town Yetholm, Kirk Yetholm, the outlying farms and the Bowmont Valley. Mail for Curr Burn was taken on foot over the hill from Halterburn. There was also a Telegram Lady (Marjorie Grahamslaw).

When the Tices moved over to the east side of the main street, the post office was taken over by people named Hedger, who also sold Hoover vacuum cleaners.

The present post office was formerly the police station, and it had cells. Two policemen I remember –Willy Morgan, who went about his business on a bicycle; and P.C. Stirling, a very serious man who drove a blue van. At Christmas times, turkey patrols were carried out, and I remember P.C. Stirling manning a road block outside the Wauchope Hall. The police station moved to the top of Dow Brae in 1969.

The Adams' shop was originally run by Mr and Mrs John Adams, who came from Fraserburgh. Their son, Alex, had a tiny shop beside Lees the butcher, selling sweets. He eventually took over his parents' shop, hence the present shop is still referred to by older citizens as "Alex's".

In the Border Boot Store, run by Mr Wakeford, I clearly remember the display counter and the smell of leather! In my memory the Misses Wait were dressmakers and their tiny shop selling newspapers, sweets, ice cream and vegetables was run by "Nessie" Abernethy. Her brother, "Mid", ran the market garden with Doddie Young, and was also one of the postmen.

I saw my first banana after the war in Hardie's the grocer. Christie's, near Gibson's Garage, was run by Francis Christie's parents, where I made "sugar castles" in the drawers in which the sugar was stored before being weighed into bags.

When I was young the village garage was on the other side of the road, on the site of what is now Douglas Gibson's property. The garage operated out of sheds and a stone building and the petrol pumps were originally hand–operated. Shortly after the present garage was built, Frank Gibson died from a heart attack while playing in the annual Yetholm Handba' game.

When the bus service was operated by S.M.T. (or latterly Eastern Scottish) the last bus overnighted in Kirk Yetholm, being parked on the Green. The bus service used to be very busy and I remember "duplicates" being run in the evening. Two buses would leave Kelso after 5 pm and when passengers got off at farms along the route, there was then need for one bus only: the two buses would stop around Greenleas/Graden and passengers would change buses and one bus would then be filled with folks on their way to Kelso. About twice a week there was a "Pictures" bus allowing people to go to the cinema in Kelso. The bus driver was in a separate cab, with the conductress in charge of the interior. One of the drivers was Bobby Blythe (Libby's father). One was Jimmy Cessford (father of George and Margaret Notman) and his conductress was Edith Young, now living in Kirk Yetholm. Another driver was Ritchie Stenhouse, who was based in Kelso and only got to drive to Yetholm as a relief driver. He was known as "Deek" (Romany for "look") because he was for ever checking his watch! Twice a week the village had a visit from a "United" bus to and from Wooler.

R & W Young, the livestock transport business ("Young's of Yetholm") may have been started before the war by the father, George. It was a big business – about ten lorries, all beautifully kept. Mainly livestock transport, but there were two specially designated horse–boxes. Robert (Bob) loved horses and drove a Jaguar; his brother, Will, lived in Woodbank Road and then moved to "Montana", where Dennis Young lives. He was a driver of one of the lorries. R & W lorries could be seen all over the country, and one seldom travelled to Edinburgh without meeting at least one of them. The lorries were kept in the long, now derelict garage near the kirk, and then in the big "new" garage in Kirk Yetholm.

Yetholm had a well known horse trainer in those days, "Buster" Fenningworth, who operated from Shotton. A string of horses being exercised was a common village sight.

I knew some of the farms very well. My memory of Venchen is of many farm cottages and bothies, with lines of men singling turnips. Probably up to a dozen men would be employed. The farm steward was Bert Guthrie. Yetholm Mains and Halterburn were farmed by the Robertons.

In the early 1960s Halterburn became a hotel run by Mr Mossman, and because of its interior design Yetholm christened it The Ponderosa after a popular American Western serial on TV called "Bonanza". Mr Mossman used to run a bus from Kelso for his customers, but the breathalyser killed the hotel. Cherrytrees was a virtual village on its own, with important owners. When I was a boy Major Marshall was the owner. A later owner was Lord Molson, a life peer, formerly MP for Derby High Peak and a minister in Harold MacMillan's government.

My memories of the church in Kirk Yetholm are that it was always full on Sundays, even the gallery. We children also attended Sunday school, where there were several classes. We were given texts to take away and memorise for the following week. The minister was the Rev. Kenneth MacFadden, an Ulsterman who, along with his wife and daughter, kept very much to themselves. We children always got the giggles when he entered the kirk, fully robed including academic hood.

Mother's ancestors were blueblood Presbyterian ministers, including two University Principals at St Andrews, one of whom, Principal Tulloch, was a Chaplain to Queen Victoria. His bust stands at the entrance to the dining room at Balmoral: Robin McHaffie saw it there some years ago after preaching at Crathie Church.

I have two books written by Principal Tulloch's son, W.W. Tulloch, who for a time was minister at Kelso Parish Church. The two books are about Queen Victoria: the first bears the Queen's handwriting in the margin, pointing out errors, and the second edition includes the corrections. Mother went to the kirk every Sunday. Father never did.

The pubs: Town Yetholm had the Plough and the Swan, both owned by Vaux of Sunderland at that time, and then there was the upmarket Romany House Hotel. The Plough and Swan bars were always busy, as was the Border in Kirk Yetholm. The Bowmont Valley farmers drove down nightly to drink and socialise. Women were not welcome in the bars for many years. The Border had a "jug and bottle", a tiny room with a counter where women could buy drink. The Border was run by Nan and Archy Donaldson, who had a tempestuous relationship, which sometimes spilled on to rows on the Green, waking the neighbourhood! Nan was very kind, and every Boxing Day gave a party for all the Kirk Yetholm children – tree, Santa, gifts and food!

Romany House Hotel in my time belonged to Mr and Mrs Semple, but I do not recall ever being inside. I always thought it attracted a "genteel" clientele, and when I was away at school I would notice adverts. for Romany in the Glasgow newspaper, *The Bulletin*. When Romany House became an old people's home it played an important part in the village as an employer. Matrons were Mrs Catherine Russell, from Morebattle, and Betty Chambers, now living in Greenlaw. My mother used to organise a rota of ladies in the village who would take the residents for drives.Village dances were very popular. The Wauchope Hall would be crammed. Men at one end, women at the other. After each dance, they would retreat to their ends again! And the gallery would be full of more mature people, watching.

So many changes, so many memories, so many people no longer here. Though the world is increasingly becoming a global village, we have to try to maintain our Scottish culture and keep Yetholm a special place.

EDITOR'S NOTE

Writing and bringing this book to publication has been very much a team effort: the text was written by more than a dozen members and supporters. The authors of articles are:

"The Very Beginning", "From Northumbrian Settlement to Scottish Border Village" and *"Hill-walking in the Cheviots"* are by David Hutchinson.

"Turbulent Times" by the late Janet Campbell

"Yetholm Loses the Working Horse" by Jonathan Parsons

"Yetholm Border Shepherds' Show" by Harry Sangster

"High Days and Holidays", "Inns and Ale Houses", "Smuggling Days" and *"Professor John Gray"* by Gordon Ogilvie

"Many More Wild Flowers Then" and *"So Many Changes in Bird Life"* by Jean Pinkney

*"A Hard Row to Hoe"*and *"The Private Fee-paying Schools"* by Pat Nicolson

"The Pennine Way", "St Cuthbert's Way" and *"The E2 Europath"* by Keith Allbeson

"Yetholm Parish Militia Club" by Andy Gray

"Roads in the Borders" by Brian Ashby

Most of the other essays were written by Bill Rae

The personal recollections of Yetholm gathered at Chapter 12 are by Alastair Turnbull, Doug Turnbull, the late Tom Smith, and the late Isa Nichol.

The rear cover is the work of Brian Ashby, as is the Turnpike Roads map. The pencil drawings are by Guy Campbell.

Bill Rae
Editor
August 2006

SELECT BIBLIOGRAPHY

Adamson and Lamont-Brown. *The Victorian and Edwardian Borderland* (Alvie Publications), St Andrews 1981

Andrew, Christopher. *Secret Service: The Making of the British Intelligence Community* (William Heinemann) London. Sceptre edition 1986.

Baird, Dr William. *Memoir of the late Rev. John Baird* (James Nisbet & Co.) London 1862.

Baird, William. *Genera Wauchope* (Oliphant Anderson and Ferrier) Edinburgh and London. Fourth Edition 1902.

Bogg, Edmund. *A Thousand Miles of Wandering in the Border Country* (Mawson, Swan and Morgan) Newcastle 1898.

Carruthers, Tom. *Golf Club Maker: Thomas Carruthers 1840-1924* (Cualann Press) Dunfermline 2004.

Douglas, Bart. Sir George. *Diversions of a Country Gentleman* (Hodder & Stoughton) London 1902.

Duerden, Frank. *The Pennine Way* (New Orchard Edition Ltd) London 1992.

Groome, Francis H. *Ordnance Gazetteer of Scotland*, New Edition (T.C. and E.C. Jack,) Edinburgh 1901. Ecclesiastical History by Rev. John Reith.

Hamilton-Edwards, Gerald. *In Search of Scottish Ancestry* (Phillimore & Co.) Chichester 1983.

Hill, C.P. *British Economic and Social History 1700-1982* (Hodder & Stoughton) London. Fifth Edition 1985.

Jeffrey, *Alexander. History and Antiquities of Roxburghshire and Adjacent Districts* (Thomas C. Jack) Edinburgh 1859

Judd, Alan. *The Quest for C* (Harper Collins) London. 2000.

Leishman, James Fleming. *Linton Leaves* (Oliver & Boyd) Edinburgh 1937.

Mackay, John James. *Border Highways* (J.J. Mackay) 1998.

Moody, David. *Scottish Local History – An Introductory Guide* (B.T. Batsford) London 1986. Pakenham, Thomas. *The Boer Wa*r (Weidenfeld and Nicolson) London 1979.

Paterson, James. *History and Genealogy of the Family of Wauchope of Niddrie-Merschell* (printed for private circulation, National Library of Scotland) 1858.

Records of Nathaniel Baird, student: Royal Scottish Academy Library, Edinburgh.

Royal Commission on the Ancient and Historic Monuments of Scotland, Roxburghshire volume (H.M.S.O.) Edinburgh 1956.

Scotland: The Blue Guides (Ernest Benn Ltd) London 1967.

Smith, Roger and Ron Shaw. *St Cuthbert's Way: Official Trail Guide* (StationeryOffice) 1997.
Statistical Accounts of Scotland
- 1791-1799. *Parish of Yetholm* by Rev. William Blackie.
- 1845. *Parish of Yetholm by Rev. John Baird* (revised 1835).
- 1952. *Parish of Yetholm* by Rev. Kenneth MacFadden.
- 1986. *Parish of Yetholm* by Rev. Joseph Brown.

Steel, *Tom. Scotland's Story: A New Perspective* (William Collins & Sons) London 1984.

Tait, James. *Two Centuries of Border Church Life* (J. and J.H. Rutherfurd) Kelso 1889.

Truckell, Alfred Edgar. Manuscript: Dumfriesshire Military Records at Dumfries County Library.

Wainwright, A. *The Pennine Way Companion* (Westmorland Gazette) Kendal 1994.

Weir, Rev Robert W. *A History of the Scottish Borderers Militia* (Dumfries Herald) 1877.

ARTICLES, PERIODICALS, MANUSCRIPTS AND MISCELLANEOUS

Beveridge, Mrs Jane. Yetholm scrapbooks, 1958-1988.

Blackwood's Edinburgh Magazine. Vol I, Issues I to VI, April-September 1817: *Notices on Scottish gipsies,* pp 43-58; 154-161; 462-465; 615-620.

Border Counties Chronicle and Mail.
Border Life, 1999.

Border Magazine. c. June 1898.

Chambers' Journal. 18 August 1883, pp 518-520.

Daily Herald. 22 June 1935.

Edinburgh Weekly Journal. 29 February 1804.

The Field. 16 November 1972.

The Great Outdoor Magazine. December 1999.

The Guardian. 2 July 2001.

The Herald. 25 April 2000.

Kelso Chronicle and Mail.

Kelso Mail. 4 October 1821; 23 February 1898; 1 June 1898.

Manuscript by Alfred Edgar Truckell, Dumfriesshire Military Records, Dumfries County Library.

National Archives of Scotland, Edinburgh: Yetholm file, CH2/671/14.

Nichol, Isa. *Memories of Yetholm* (unpublished) c.1963

Papers of Nathaniel Baird, Royal Scottish Academy Library, Edinburgh.

The People's Journal. October 1927.

Pigot's Directory (Pigot & Co.), 1825-1826, pp 655-656.

Royal Infirmary of Edinburgh Annual Report, 1864-1865.

Scots Magazine:
- Daw, Arthur. 'A Fond Look Back at Yetholm' March 1978, pp 577-585. 'We Didn't Need Street Names Then' April 1978, pp 66-75
- Gray, Rev. Professor John. 'Dear Old Kirk Yetholm!' February 1962, pp 406-415. 'The Man From Bowmont Water' February 1973, pp 479-485.

The Scotsman (letter, date unknown), 1937; and 11 December 1999.

Scottish Office. Report of Public Local Inquiry re Myrtle Cottage, Main Street,Town Yetholm, September 1992.

Southern Counties Register and Directory (J. and J.H. Rutherfurd) Kelso 1866, pp 156-162.

The Southern Reporter (early1934; August 1960 and October 1961).

Wauchope Hall minute book, 1919-1954.

Yetholm Border Shepherds' Show minute books, etc. 1926-1980.

Yetholm Cricket Club minute book, 1884-1924.

Yetholm Parish Council Minute Books: 1884-1890, 1897-1930: Scottish Borders Archive, Selkirk: file R/PR/1/26.

Yetholm Parish Militia Club Account Book (containing Minutes, Laws and Membership Lists of the Club) , 1820-1831: Scottish Borders Archive, Selkirk, File SC/R/56/1.

Yetholm Parish School Log 1865-1869, National Archives of Scotland, Edinburgh: Yetholm file, CH2/671/14.